sickness metaphors = lo

Gret 164

Social Issues
in Literature

Corruption in William
Shakespeare's *Hamlet*

Other Books in the Social Issues in Literature Series:

Abuse of Power in George Orwell's *Nineteen Eighty-Four*

American Dream/Alienation in John Steinbeck's *Of Mice and Men*

Bioethics in Aldous Huxley's *Brave New World*

The Environment in Henry David Thoreau's *Walden*

Male/Female Roles in Ernest Hemingway's *The Sun Also Rises*

Patriarchy in Sandra Cisneros's *The House on Mango Street*

Political Issues in J.K. Rowling's Harry Potter Series

Race Relations in Alan Paton's *Cry, the Beloved Country*

Suicide in Arthur Miller's *Death of a Salesman*

War in Stephen Crane's *The Red Badge of Courage*

Women's Issues in Amy Tan's *The Joy Luck Club*

Social Issues
in Literature

Corruption in William
Shakespeare's *Hamlet*

Vernon Elso Johnson, Book Editor

GREENHAVEN PRESS
A part of Gale, Cengage Learning

Detroit • New York • San Francisco • New Haven, Conn • Waterville, Maine • London

Christine Nasso, *Publisher*
Elizabeth Des Chenes, *Managing Editor*

© 2010 Greenhaven Press, a part of Gale, Cengage Learning

Gale and Greenhaven Press are registered trademarks used herein under license.

For more information, contact:
Greenhaven Press
27500 Drake Rd.
Farmington Hills, MI 48331-3535
Or you can visit our Internet site at gale.cengage.com

Articles in Greenhaven Press anthologies are often edited for length to meet page requirements. In addition, original titles of these works are changed to clearly present the main thesis and to explicitly indicate the author's opinion. Every effort is made to ensure that Greenhaven Press accurately reflects the original intent of the authors. Every effort has been made to trace the owners of copyrighted material.

Cover image copyright Gian Correa Salero, 2009. Used under license from Shutterstock.com.

LIBRARY OF CONGRESS CATALOGING-IN-PUBLICATION DATA

Corruption in William Shakespeare's Hamlet / Vernon Elso Johnson, book editor.
    p. cm. -- (Social issues in literature)
    Includes bibliographical references and index.
    ISBN 978-0-7377-4809-3 (hardcover) -- ISBN 978-0-7377-4810-9 (pbk.)
    1. Shakespeare, William, 1564-1616. Hamlet. 2. Hamlet (Legendary character)--
Juvenile literature. 3. Political corruption in literature--Juvenile literature. I.
Johnson, Vernon E. (Vernon Elso), 1921-
    PR2807.C66 2010
    822.3'3--dc22
                                                                2009041881

Printed in the United States of America
2 3 4 5 6 7 14 13 12 11 10

Contents

Introduction   9

Chronology   12

Chapter 1: The Background of William Shakespeare

1. The Educated Man   16

   John F. Andrews

   Shakespeare's father, John Shakespeare, was able to provide his son with a superior classical education (though
   not university training).

2. Religion, Grief, and Suicide   27

   Peter Holland

   Shakespeare's familiarity with Catholic doctrine regarding last rites and suicide, and his struggle with grief, can
   be seen in the burial of Ophelia.

3. The Death of a Son and a Father   35

   G.B. Harrison

   The death of Shakespeare's son Hamnet could have led
   him to write the play *Hamlet* as a memorial to his child.

Chapter 2: The Issue of Corruption in *Hamlet*

1. Corruption in Denmark   43

   A.C. Bradley

   The corruption of Claudius and others is present from
   the first and becomes clearer with his suspicion of Hamlet in Act II. The hand of Providence is seen throughout.

2. Politics in *Hamlet*   52

   John Erskine Hankins

   Parallels between corruption in *Hamlet*'s Denmark and
   Elizabethan England would have been readily apparent to
   the play's audience.

3. Sickness in Denmark   **61**
   Caroline F.E. Spurgeon

   Sickness and disease in *Hamlet* are symbols of inner psychological corruption and outer political corruption.

4. Claudius Turns the World Mad   **68**
   Andrew Gurr

   Claudius has created a corrupt world in which decent values have been turned upside-down and members of families and the court have been driven insane.

5. Corruption Is a Progressive, Pervasive Disease   **74**
   Derek Antona Traversi

   Both Claudius and Hamlet spread disease with their murders, spying, and cruelty, until death takes the lives of most of the characters at the end.

6. Hamlet Is Corrupt, Not Claudius   **82**
   G. Wilson Knight

   Because of Claudius's actions, Hamlet becomes the real poison in the kingdom.

7. The Corruption of Reason   **90**
   Juliet McLauchlan

   Hamlet's reason and values might at first have healed Denmark's disease, but by the end, the situation is too hopeless for even reason to put things right.

8. Corruption's Effect on Love   **99**
   H.D.F. Kitto

   Hamlet, like Greek drama, is religious in nature, and shows the destruction of the greatest good: love itself.

9. Corruption Destroys a Generation   **107**
   Margreta de Grazia

   Claudius, with the collaboration of Polonius and older courtiers, destroyed not only the kingdom of Denmark but also the younger generation, which should have been coming to power.

Chapter 3: Corruption in the Twenty-first Century

1. Corruption Creates Economic Inequality   **115**
   Daniel Brook
   Billions of dollars are easily available to the wealthiest among us at the expense of the majority of Americans.

2. Corruption in a Global Corporate Empire   **125**
   Paul Kingsnorth
   International corporate crime damages every segment of the global population.

3. Corruption and the Pentagon   **128**
   Pratap Chatterjee
   Inflated no-bid military contracts have been awarded to former vice president Dick Cheney's company, Halliburton, and its associates, at the expense of soldiers and foreign workers.

4. Torture and Espionage   **138**
   Democracy Now!
   A "Truth Commission" has been formed to look into the George W. Bush administration's policies of detention, torture, and domestic spying.

5. Exploiting Clients and Third World Countries   **146**
   Ron Scherer and Brendan Conway
   Robert Allen Stanford, who owns airlines, newspapers, and banks, has been charged with fraud.

6. Justice Politicized   **152**
   David Iglesias with Davin Seay
   Iglesias, one of seven judges fired for political reasons alone, examines corruption in the Department of Justice.

For Further Discussion   **162**

For Further Reading   **163**

Bibliography   **164**

Index   **166**

Introduction

At the turn of the seventeenth century, William Shakespeare dropped into a very dark mood, induced perhaps by personal tensions and a sense of national malaise. The century was marked by violent religious wars and endless attempts to seize the English throne. The Protestant Reformation produced not only wars of unsurpassed cruelty but also intense struggles concerning legitimate succession to the English throne at a time when England stood in danger of being absorbed by Spain or France. Henry VIII's devoutly Catholic daughter, Mary Tudor, or "Bloody Mary," as she was called, attempted with persecutions and deaths to make England Catholic; then, her sister, Elizabeth, who succeeded Mary, approved Parliament's Act of Uniformity, requiring all Englishmen to conform to the Church of England, which resulted in official persecutions of Catholics. All these factors seriously affected the life of John Shakespeare, Shakespeare's father, who was a suspected Catholic. This, in turn, affected the life and career of Shakespeare.

Early in 1601, when Shakespeare was supposedly still working changes into *Hamlet*, a series of dramatic events took place that complicated his view of corruption and affected him deeply. In late February, Robert Devereux, the Earl of Essex, a young man for whom Elizabeth had shown great affection, attempted to seize the throne by force. He was caught, convicted of treason, and executed—inside the Tower rather than outside, so that mobs could create no disturbances in his favor. One of Devereux's followers in this was the Earl of Southampton, a patron of the Globe Theatre, in which Shakespeare had a financial interest. As a final gesture, to throw the fear of God—and of government—into one and all, Devereux's rotting head was displayed at the Tower for a year afterward. Also wounding Shakespeare deeply in this period was the death in 1596 of his young son, Hamnet, whom he had left behind with the rest of his family in Stratford to pursue a career in London—a death that lingered passionately in his mind.

In this same period of shifting reality, Shakespeare produced *Hamlet*, probing into the dark recesses of the human soul and showing how corruption—"rottenness"—spreads through the realm of Denmark following the crimes of Claudius, much like the plague, which periodically closed all London theaters. Despite all this, however, or perhaps because of it, in this period Shakespeare achieved unsurpassed mastery of the dramatic form.

Shakespeare had dealt with all such issues before—in the English history plays, which included all the corruption that surfaced in *Hamlet*—but never with such a psychological sense of brilliance and darkness. In *Richard II* the man who became Henry IV forcibly deposes Richard and then takes his throne, after which one character prophecies that "the blood of English shall manure the ground and future ages groan for this foul act." This act thus precipitates a curse that, as in *Hamlet*, endures until the evil has worked itself out. Ironically, this play, too, entered into the Essex scandal. Supporters of Essex persuaded the Globe to revive *Richard II* on the day before the planned coup, supposedly under the belief that this display of a "peaceful" usurpation and the following announcement of an accomplished fact would ease acceptance by the public. As a result, the Globe actors were arrested and questioned but then released. Shakespeare also at the end of his career wrote *Henry VIII*, about the English king who, on the day before he was crowned, married his dead brother's widow to help cement his power.

The dark and probing view of mankind that began with *Hamlet* continued with *Troilus and Cressida*, a Trojan War story with a scathing view of war and the lust of its heroine, who betrays her vows to leap into the arms of a Greek warrior—much like Hamlet's view of his mother's marriage to Claudius. Then followed *King Lear,* in which two daughters fight brutally for power; *Macbeth,* again showing regicide and lust for power; and, at the end of his tragic period, *Coriolanus,* a story of arrogance and murder with no final justice at the end.

Several literary and philosophical traditions of the time also played a role in *Hamlet.* In form, it is a "revenge tragedy," a type popularized by Thomas Kyd's *The Spanish Tragedy,* but actually dating back to the Roman playwright/philosopher Seneca, who was studied by English schoolboys and who contributed the use of ghosts, violence on stage, and the five-act structure to the English theater. Philosophically, *Hamlet* reflects the growing ideas of the Renaissance, as illustrated by the moral humanism of Erasmus; the skepticism of Montaigne, whose motto was "What do I know?"; and the cynical views of Machiavelli, who advised that the ideal prince should be purely utilitarian, regardless of morality.

The studies of Shakespeare and *Hamlet* included here approach the issue of corruption on multiple levels and different points of view. Chapter 1 deals with pertinent events in Shakespeare's life, while Chapter 1 presents critical studies of corruption in a universally mysterious play. In Chapter 3 today's writers comment on massive corruption in the twenty-first century, especially in government and multinational corporations.

Chronology

1564

William Shakespeare is born in Stratford-upon-Avon.

1568

John Shakespeare, Shakespeare's father, is elected bailiff, but rumors that he is a secret Catholic damage his standing in the community.

1576

The Theatre (the first professional theater) opens north of London.

1582

William Shakespeare marries Anne Hathaway.

1583

Shakespeare's daughter Susanna is born.

1585

Shakespeare's twins, Hamnet and Judith, are born.

c. 1588–1589

Shakespeare goes to London without his family. His first plays are performed.

1590–1596

Shakespeare writes *The Comedy of Errors*, three parts of *Henry VI*, *Venus and Adonis*, *The Rape of Lucrece*, *The Taming of the Shrew*, *The Two Gentlemen of Verona*, *Richard III*, *Romeo and Juliet*, *Richard II*, *King John*, *A Midsummer Night's Dream*, and *Love's Labour's Lost*.

1593–1594

Shakespeare acquires a share in the Lord Chamberlain's Men, beginning a successful career as an investor in theaters.

1596

Shakespeare's son, Hamnet, dies at age eleven.

1597

The Merchant of Venice and *Henry IV, Part I* are produced, and Shakespeare invests in property in Stratford.

1598–1600

Henry IV, Part 2, As You Like It, Much Ado About Nothing, The Merry Wives of Windsor, Henry V, and *Julius Caesar* are presented. Shakespeare's company moves to the Globe Theatre.

c. 1601–1602

Hamlet is completed, though some scholars believe Shakespeare continued to make changes as late as 1604. The folio contained further changes.

1601

Shakespeare's father dies after much financial trouble.

1602

Twelfth Night is produced.

1604

Measure for Measure and *Othello* are produced.

1605–1606

King Lear is produced, and *Macbeth* is presumably presented before James I.

1606–1611

Pericles is performed at court. *Antony and Cleopatra, Coriolanus, The Winter's Tale, The Tempest,* and *Cymbeline* are staged.

1608

Shakespeare's mother, Mary Arden Shakespeare, dies.

1609

Shakespeare's company purchases Blackfriars Theatre.

c. 1612

Shakespeare moves to Stratford-upon-Avon.

1613

Henry VIII is produced, and the Globe is destroyed by fire, possibly ignited during a production of *Henry VIII*. It reopens the following year.

1616

Shakespeare dies.

1623

Anne Hathaway dies. Shakespeare's friends publish thirty-six of his plays, an edition known as the First Folio.

The Background of William Shakespeare

The Educated Man

John F. Andrews ⋏⋏ Ƨ.Ƒ.?

John F. Andrews is an editor, scholar, critic, and founder of the Shakespeare Guild. He has taught at several American universities.

Andrews, providing the important features of William Shakespeare's life, covers his birth, his parent's position in Stratford, his education, his courtship and marriage to Anne Hathaway, his subsequent career in London, and his death. Seven years after his death, two of his friends paid tribute to him by publishing his collected works. Shakespeare's father, John Shakespeare, was an uneducated tradesman, ambitious for social status and money. Because of his various public positions, he was able to enroll Shakespeare in a local school where he received an excellent education. Though Shakespeare did not attend university, he was trained in Latin and Greek, which find their way into his plays. Shakespeare's theatrical experience—as writer, actor, director, and producer—gave him a thorough command of acting, stage craft, and the Elizabethan audience.

One thing we do know is that if Shakespeare was a man for all time, he was also very much a man of his own age. Christened at Holy Trinity Church in Stratford-upon-Avon on 26 April 1564, he grew up as the eldest of five children reared by John Shakespeare, a tradesman who played an increasingly active role in the town's civic affairs as his business prospered, and Mary Arden Shakespeare, the daughter of a gentleman farmer from nearby Wilmcote. Whether Shakespeare was born on 23 April, as tradition holds, is not known; but a birth date only a few days prior to the recorded baptism

John F. Andrews, *Dictionary of Literary Biography, Vol. 62: Elizabethan Dramatists.* Belmont, CA: Gale Research Company, 1987. Copyright © 1987 Gale Research Company. Reproduced by permission of Gale, a part of Cengage Learning.

seems eminently probable, particularly in view of the fear his parents must have had that William, like two sisters who had preceded him and one who followed, might die in infancy. By the time young William was old enough to begin attending school, he had a younger brother (Gilbert, born in 1566) and a baby sister (Joan, born in 1569). As he attained his youth, he found himself with two more brothers to help look after (Richard, born in 1574, and Edmund, born in 1580), the younger of whom eventually followed his by-then-prominent eldest brother to London and the theater, where he had a brief career as an actor before his untimely death at twenty-seven.

Shakespeare's Father

The house where Shakespeare spent his childhood stood adjacent to the wool shop in which his father plied a successful trade as a glover and dealer in leather goods and other commodities. Before moving to Stratford sometime prior to 1552 (when the records show that he was fined for failing to remove a dunghill from outside his house to the location where refuse was normally to be deposited), John Shakespeare had been a farmer in the neighboring village of Snitterfield. Whether he was able to read and write is uncertain. He executed official documents, not with his name, but with a cross signifying his glover's compasses. Some scholars interpret this as a "signature" that might have been considered more "authentic" than a full autograph; others have taken it to be an indication of illiteracy. But even if John Shakespeare was not one of the "learned," he was certainly a man of what a later age would call upward mobility. By marrying Mary Arden, the daughter of his father's landlord, he acquired the benefits of a better social standing and a lucrative inheritance, much of which he invested in property (he bought several houses). And by involving himself in public service, he rose by sure degrees to the highest municipal positions Stratford had to offer: chamberlain (1561), alderman (1565), and bailiff (or mayor) and justice of the peace (1568). A few years after his elevation to the office of bailiff, probably around 1576, John Shakespeare approached the College of Heralds for armorial bearings and the right to call himself a gentleman. Before his application was acted upon, however, his fortunes took a sudden turn for the worse, and it was not until 1596, when his eldest son had attained some status and renewed the petition, that a Shakespeare coat of arms was finally granted. This must have been a comfort to John Shakespeare in his declining years (he died in 1601), because by then he had borrowed money, disposed of property out of necessity, ceased to attend meetings of the town council, become involved in litigation and been assessed fines, and even stopped attending church services, for fear, it was said, "of process for debt." Just what happened to alter John Shakespeare's financial and social position after the mid 1570s is not clear. Some have seen his nonattendance at church as a sign that he had become a recusant, unwilling to conform to the practices of the newly established Church of England (his wife's family had remained loyal to Roman Catholicism despite the fact that the old faith was under vigorous attack in Warwickshire after 1577), but the scant surviving evidence is anything but definitive.

Shakespeare's Education

The records we do have suggest that during young William's formative years he enjoyed the advantages that would have accrued to him as the son of one of the most influential citizens of a bustling market town in the fertile Midlands. When he was taken to services at Holy Trinity Church, he would have sat with his family in the front pew, in accordance with his father's civic rank. There he would have heard and felt the words and rhythms of the Bible, the sonorous phrases of the 1559 Book of Common Prayer, the exhortations of the Homilies. In all likelihood, after spending a year or two at a "petty school" to learn the rudiments of reading and writing, he

William Shakespeare (1564–1616), the renowned English poet, playwright, and author of Hamlet.

would have proceeded, at the age of seven, to "grammar school." Given his father's social position, young William would have been eligible to attend the King's New School, located above the Guild Hall and adjacent to the Guild Chapel (institutions that would both have been quite familiar to a man with the elder Shakespeare's municipal duties), no more than a five-minute walk from the Shakespeare house on Henley Street. Though no records survive to tell us who attended the Stratford grammar school during this period, we do know that it had well-qualified and comparatively well-paid masters; and, through the painstaking research of such scholars as T.W. Baldwin, we now recognize that a curriculum such as the one offered at the King's New School would have equipped its pupils with what by modern standards would be a rather formidable classical education.

During his many long school days there, young Shakespeare would have become thoroughly grounded in Latin, acquired some background in Greek, and developed enough linguistic facility to pick up whatever he may have wanted later from such modern languages as Italian and French. Along the way he would have become familiar with such authors as Aesop, Caesar, Cicero, Sallust, Livy, Virgil, Horace, Ovid, and Seneca. He would have studied logic and rhetoric as well as grammar, and he would have been taught the principles of composition and oratory from the writings of such masters as Quintilian and Erasmus. In all probability, he would even have received some training in speech and drama through the performance of plays by Plautus and Terence. If Shakespeare's references to schooling and schoolmasters in the plays are a reliable index of how he viewed his own years as a student, we must conclude that the experience was more tedious than pleasurable. But it is difficult to imagine a more suitable mode of instruction for the formation of a Renaissance poet's intellectual and artistic sensibility. . . .

Married Life and London Career

Once his school years ended, Shakespeare married, at eighteen, a woman who was eight years his senior. We know that Anne Hathaway was pregnant when the marriage license was issued by the Bishop of Worcester on 27 November 1582, because a daughter, Susanna, was baptized in Holy Trinity six months later on 26 May 1583. We have good reason to believe that the marriage was hastily arranged: there was only one reading of the banns (a church announcement preceding a wedding that allowed time for any legal impediments against it to be brought forward before the ceremony took place), an indication of unusual haste. But whether the marriage was in any way "forced" is impossible to determine. . . .

What we do have to go on is certainly compatible with the suspicion that William and Anne were somewhat less than ardent lovers. They had only two more children—the twins, Hamnet and Judith, baptized on 2 February 1585—and they lived more than a hundred miles apart, so far as we can tell, for the better part of the twenty-year period during which Shakespeare was employed in the London theater. If we can give any credence to an amusing anecdote recorded in the 1602–1603 diary of a law student named John Manningham, there was at least one occasion during those years when Shakespeare, overhearing the actor Richard Burbage make an assignation, "went before, was entertained, and at his game before Burbage came; then, message being brought that Richard the Third was at the door, Shakespeare caused return to be made that William the Conqueror was before Richard the Third." If we read the sonnets as in any way autobiographical, moreover, we are shown a poet with at least one other significant liaison: a "Dark Lady" to whom Will's lust impels him despite the self-disgust the affair arouses in him (and despite her infidelity with the fair "Young Man" to whom many of the poems are addressed and for whom the poet reserves his deepest feelings). . . .

If we look at what Shakespeare had written by the early 1590s, we see that he had already become thoroughly familiar with the daily round of one of the great capitals of Europe. Shakespeare knew St. Paul's Cathedral, famous not only as a house of worship but also as the marketplace where books were bought and sold. He knew the Inns of Court, where aspiring young lawyers studied for the bar. He knew the river Thames, spanned by the ever-busy, ever-fascinating London Bridge. He knew the Tower, where so many of the characters he would depict in his history plays had met their deaths, and where in his own lifetime such prominent noblemen as the Earl of Essex and Sir Walter Raleigh would be imprisoned prior to their executions. He knew Westminster, where Parliament met when summoned by the Queen, and where the Queen herself held court at Whitehall Palace. He knew the harbor, where English ships, having won control of the seas by defeating the "invincible" Spanish Armada in 1588, had begun in earnest to explore the New World.

In Shakespeare's day London was a vigorous city of somewhere between 150,000 and 200,000 inhabitants. If in its more majestic aspects it was dominated by the court of Queen Elizabeth, in its everyday affairs it was accented by the hustle and bustle of getting and spending. Its Royal Exchange was one of the forerunners of today's stock exchanges. Its many market-places offered a variety of goods for a variety of tastes. Its crowded streets presented a colorful pageant of Elizabethan modes of transport and dress, ranging from countrywomen in homespun to elegant ladies in apparel as decorative as their husbands' wealth—and the Queen's edicts on clothing—would allow. Its inns and taverns afforded a rich diversity of vivid personalities—eating, tippling, chatting, and enjoying games and pleasures of all kinds. It was in short, an immensely stimulating social and cultural environment, and we can be sure that Shakespeare took full advantage of the opportunity it gave him to observe humanity in all its facets. . . .

Professional Experience

Shakespeare's position with [the theatrical group] the Lord Chamberlain's Men was a source of professional stability that probably had a great deal to do with his growth and maturation as a writer. For one thing, it freed him from some of the uncertainties and frustrations that must have been the lot of other playwrights, virtually all of whom operated as free-lancers selling their wares to impresarios such as Philip Henslowe (often for as little as five pounds), and most of whom thus forfeited any real say about how their plays were to be produced and, in time (if a given acting company so wished or if chance provided), published. From at least 1594 on Shakespeare was a stockholder of the theatrical organization for which he wrote his plays. After 1598 (when the sons of the recently deceased James Burbage, Cuthbert and Richard, invited four of the principal actors in the Lord Chamberlain's Men to become their partners and put up half the capital needed to rebuild the Theatre across the Thames as the Globe), Shakespeare was also a co-owner of the playhouse in which that company performed the plays. As such, he shared in all the profits the Lord Chamberlain's Men took in at the gate, and he was undoubtedly a participant in most, if not all, of the major decisions affecting the company's welfare. We know from the surviving legal records of the playwright's various business transactions that he prospered financially by this arrangement: like his father, Shakespeare invested wisely in real estate, purchasing properties in both Stratford and London. And we can infer from the evidence of his rapidly developing sophistication as a dramatist that Shakespeare's membership in a close-knit group of theatrical entrepreneurs also helped him flourish artistically.

It meant, for example, that he could envisage and write his plays with particular performers in mind: Richard Burbage for leading roles such as Richard III, Othello, and King Lear; Will Kempe for clowning parts such as Launce or Dogberry in the early years of the company, and thereafter (following Kempe's departure from the Lord Chamberlain's Men around 1599) Robert Armin, who seems to have specialized in "wise fools" such as Touchstone, Feste, and Lear's Fool; Shakespeare himself, perhaps, for "old men" such as Adam in *As You Like It*; "hired men" (adult actors who, not being shareholders in the company, were simply paid a sum of money for each job of work) for most of the lesser roles; and apprentice boy-actors for the youthful parts and many, if not all, of the female roles (there being no actresses on the English stage until the theaters reopened after the Restoration). Working as the resident playwright for a company in which he was both an actor and a business partner meant that Shakespeare could revise and rewrite his scripts in rehearsal prior to a given play's first performance, and that he could adapt and further revise them later as differing circumstances required: such as performances commissioned at Court during holiday seasons or on ceremonial occasions, or performances solicited by the great houses of the nobility, or (during sieges of plague when the London theaters were closed) performances on tour in the provinces, during which, in all likelihood, the troupe was reduced to entertaining with fewer actors and was required to make do with provisional playing areas in guild halls, inn yards, and other less-than-ideal theatrical spaces.

Because the conditions under which Shakespeare worked required him, above all, to be pragmatic and flexible, we would probably be correct to infer that as he composed his plays he thought of his scripts, not as fixed "literary" texts, but as provisional production notes—susceptible of lengthening or shortening or other modes of alteration as determined by the constraints of particular venues and performance situations. He would have had to prepare each script with an eye to the number of actors available for speaking parts (one recent scholar has concluded that most of Shakespeare's plays were composed with a cast of thirteen performers in mind), and he probably planned each scene with a view to the possibilities for "doubling" (a principle of theatrical economy whereby a given actor would alternate among two or more roles in the same play). It may well be that, in the absence of anyone else in the organization designated to function in that capacity, Shakespeare was the first "director" his plays had. If so, we can be sure that he approached the task with an awareness that the devising of a production was a collaborative process and that the playscript, though normative, was never to be revered as a monument carved in stone. Shakespeare was, after all, a *playwright* (that is, a "maker" rather than merely a writer of plays), and he would have been the first to recognize that the final purpose of a dramatic text was a fully realized performance rather than a piece of literature to be read in the privacy of a patron's parlor or pondered in the lamplight of a scholar's study. . . .

Shakespeare's Final Years

Tradition holds that Shakespeare returned to Stratford for his declining years, and three years after the burning of the Globe his own flame went out. Following his death on 23 April 1616, he was laid to rest where fifty-two years earlier he had been christened. Shortly thereafter, a monument to his memory was erected above the tomb in Holy Trinity, and that monument is still in place for Shakespeare admirers to see today. But an even greater monument to his memory appeared seven years later, when his theatrical colleagues, John Heminge and Henry Condell (both of whom had been mentioned in the playwright's will) assembled a large volume of his collected plays. The 1623 First Folio was a labor of love, compiled as "an office to the dead, to procure his orphans guardians" and "to keep the memory of so worthy a friend and fellow alive as was our Shakespeare."

Our Shakespeare. It is not without exaggeration that the book that preserves what is probably his most reliable portrait and the most authoritative versions of the majority of his dramatic texts (indeed the *only* surviving versions of half of them) has been called "incomparably the most important work in the English language." In the words and actions that fill his poems and plays, in the performances that enrich our theaters and silver screens, in the countless off-shoots to be found in other works of art, and in the influence the playwright continues to have on virtually every aspect of popular culture throughout the world, now as much as in the age of Elizabeth and James, Shakespeare lives.

Religion, Grief, and Suicide

Peter Holland

Peter Holland, an internationally acclaimed Shakespeare scholar, is McMeel Family Professor of Shakespeare Studies at the University of Notre Dame and editor of the Shakespeare Survey.

William Shakespeare's father's troublesome relationship to the Catholic Church can be seen in Hamlet *in the grumblings over burying Ophelia, a suicide, in holy ground, argues Holland in the following selection. Shakespeare and Anne Hathaway had three children, the last two being twins, Hamnet and Judith, named for friends in Stratford. In 1596, the death of Hamnet intensified portrayals of grief in the plays that followed, especially* Hamlet, *about a son's grief for a father. The death of Ophelia, Holland asserts, seems to have been influenced by the inquest in 1579 of a young woman named Katherine Hamlett.*

Shakespeare, William (1564–1616), playwright and poet, was baptized, probably by the parish priest, John Bretchgirdle, in Holy Trinity, the parish church of Stratford upon Avon, on 26 April 1564, the third child of John Shakespeare (d. 1601) and Mary Arden (d. 1608). It seems appropriate that the first of many gaps in the records of his life should be the exact date of Shakespeare's birth, though that is a common problem for the period. He was probably born on 21, 22, or 23 April 1564, given the 1559 prayer book's instructions to parents on the subject of baptisms. But, ever since Joseph Greene, an eighteenth-century Stratford curate, informed the scholar George Steevens that Shakespeare was born on 23 April, with no apparent evidence for his assertion, and Steevens adopted that date in his 1773 edition of Shakespeare, it has been usual

Peter Holland, *Oxford Dictionary of National Biography: From the Earliest Times to the Year 2000*, vol. 49. Oxford: Oxford University Press, 2004. Copyright © 2004 Oxford University Press. Reproduced by permission of Oxford University Press.

to assume that Shakespeare was born on St George's day, so that England's patron saint and the birth of the 'national poet' can be celebrated on the same day. Where he was born is clearer: in 1564 his parents appear to have been living in Henley Street, probably in part of the building now known as Shakespeare's Birthplace but, equally probably, not in that part of the building in which the room traditionally known as the place of Shakespeare's birth is located. The accretion of myth and commerce around Shakespeare's biography and its material legacy produces such paradoxes. . . .

Shakespeare's Family's Status

By the time [John Shakespeare] married Mary Arden (some time between November 1556 and 1558), he had established himself in Stratford as a glover and whittawer (a dresser of light-coloured leather). He lived in Henley Street, buying a house and garden there in 1556 and starting to buy further property in town. In this he might well have been helped by his wife's inheritance: in Robert Arden's will of November 1556 she was named one of the two executors and supervised the substantial inventory of his goods and moveables in December 1556 after his death. She also inherited the valuable estate in Wilmcote known as Asbies, land that on her marriage came to her husband.

John and Mary Shakespeare were probably married in Aston Cantlow, the parish church for Wilmcote and the place where Robert Arden wanted to be buried. The exact date of the wedding is unknown but their first child, Joan, was born in September 1558 (and may well have died in infancy); Margaret was baptized in December 1562 and was buried the following April. A year later William was born. He survived the devastating plague that killed one in eight of the town's population later the same year. There were five more children: Gilbert (1566–1612), another Joan (born 1569, indicating that John and Mary's first child must have died by that year; she was the only sibling to outlive William, dying in 1646), Anne (1571–1579), Richard (1574–1613), and Edmund (1580–1607). All but Anne lived to adulthood. William's childhood was thus spent in a steadily increasing family and there were other relatives nearby: his uncle Henry Shakespeare, John's brother, lived in Snitterfield and many of his mother's sisters married local men.

John Shakespeare bought more property in Stratford in 1575, almost certainly including the rest of the 'Birthplace', creating a substantial house which even though it incorporated space for his workshop amounted to a fine home for his expanding family. But this period was also one of ever-increasing civic importance for John Shakespeare. He had risen through the lesser offices of the borough and, by the time of William's birth, was one of the fourteen burgesses of Stratford. In 1565 he became an alderman and in 1568 was elected bailiff for the year, the highest office in the town. In 1571 he became chief alderman and deputy bailiff. At about this time he also seems to have applied for a coat of arms. The family's wealth was also growing and the civic importance and high social standing that John Shakespeare had achieved in a brief period provided the context for William's upbringing.

But in the following years something seems to have gone wrong with John Shakespeare's finances. At the start of the 1570s he was stretching his commercial activities beyond his trade, dealing illegally in wool and also being prosecuted for usury [making loans and charging unfair interest]. By the end of the decade he was in debt; in 1578 he mortgaged some of Mary's inheritance and lost it in 1580 when he could not repay the sum, land that would otherwise have been inherited by William in due course. He stopped attending council meetings after 1576 as well, and was replaced as an alderman in 1586. All of this too provided a family context for William's youth; the decline in John Shakespeare's fortunes cannot have been unaccompanied by anxiety.

Ophelia, a central character in Hamlet, *is depicted floating in a river after her suicide in this 1852 John Everett Millais painting. Historians speculate that Shakespeare's writings were often inspired by actual events, such as the drowning of Katherine Hamlett in 1579.* Copyright © Tate Gallery, London/Art Resource, NY.

The Catholic Issue

In 1592 John was listed by the presenters for the parish of Stratford upon Avon as an obstinate recusant [dissenter against the Church of England], among nine on the list whose absence was identified by the presenters and by the commissioners to whom they reported as being 'for feare of processe for Debtte'. . . . There is no self-evident reason to distrust this statement, though it has been seen as an excuse to cover secret Catholicism. Certainly some Catholics feigned debt as a reason for recusancy but John Shakespeare's debts seem real enough.

In 1790 a bricklayer was reported as having found in 1757 in the roof of the Henley Street house a manuscript now known as John Shakespeare's spiritual testament. Blank copies of this formulaic document, based on one written by Cardinal [Charles] Borromeo, are claimed to have been circulated in large numbers by Catholic missionaries; this copy was said to have been completed by or on behalf of John Shakespeare. Transcribed by the great Shakespeare scholar Edmond Malone, who later came to doubt its authenticity, it is now lost and its link to John Jordan, a Stratford man well known for inventing materials to satisfy the increasing thirst for Shakespeariana, puts it under suspicion. In the unlikely event that it was genuine it would suggest that John Shakespeare was a Catholic still holding to his original faith and that William was brought up in a household where the double standards of adequate outward observance of protestant orthodoxy and private heterodoxy were largely achieved. There is, of course, no reason to assume that the adult William shared his father's religious views, and the evidence for John's being a Catholic is very far from decisive. It was, after all, during John Shakespeare's time as bailiff in 1568 that the images of the last judgment that decorated the guild chapel in Stratford were whitewashed and defaced as no longer acceptable to state protestantism, though this might simply have been a further example of John's outward conformism.

First Views of Professional Theatre

In any case, another event during John Shakespeare's tenure as bailiff seems more significant for his son's future career: the visit to Stratford of two theatre companies, the Queen's Players and Worcester's Men, the first time theatre companies are known to have played in Stratford. Since the first performance in any town was usually in front of the town officials, John Shakespeare would have seen the performances and William might well have accompanied him (as other children certainly did in similar circumstances). Further visits followed: Leicester's Men in 1572 and 1576, Warwick's Men in 1574, Worcester's Men in 1574 and 1581, Lord Strange's Men in 1578, Essex's Men in 1578 and 1583, Derby's Men in 1579, Lord Berkeley's Men in 1580 and 1582. Across the period when William was likely to have been continuously resident in Stratford, there were at least thirteen visits by companies of players, bringing a fairly wide repertory of drama, little of which can be confidently identified. None the less, there is a context there for William Shakespeare's early learning about theatre performance and contemporary drama in the work of such professional companies. He might, too, have travelled nearby to see the spectacular entertainments at Kenilworth given by the earl of Leicester for the queen in 1575, or the magnificent cycle drama of mystery plays which was still performed annually at Coventry until 1578, or Coventry's Hocktide play (suppressed in 1568 but performed again at Kenilworth in 1575), or the amateur performances which regularly occurred in Stratford. . . .

Marriage to Anne Hathaway

On 27 November a marriage licence was issued for Shakespeare's marriage to Anne Hathaway (1555/6–1623) (though the record in the bishop of Worcester's feaster mistakenly refers to the bride as Anne Whateley of Temple Grafton) and on the following day a bond was issued binding Fulke Sandells and John Richardson for the sum of £40 as surety for the marriage, a necessary step since William was at eighteen still a minor and needed his father's consent to the match. . . .

Six months after the marriage, on 26 May 1583, Susanna Shakespeare was baptized, followed on 2 February 1585 by William's and Anne's twins, Hamnet and Judith, probably named after Hamnet and Judith Sadler. Hamnet Sadler, a local baker, was in 1616 one of the witnesses of Shakespeare's will, and his name also appears in local records as Hamlet. With these three children Shakespeare's family seems to have been complete: there are no records of further children. Some have used this as evidence that the marriage was distant or unhappy, though many happily married couples both then and later have had no children at all and it is perhaps relevant that Susanna and Judith had few children (one and three respectively). . . .

Theatre Career in London

When Shakespeare became a player is not clear but it is at least possible that he joined the Queen's Men. They played in Stratford in 1587 and their repertory included a play based on Montemayor's *Diana* (the source for Shakespeare's *The Two Gentlemen of Verona*), anonymous plays on the reigns of King John (*The Troublesome Reign*), Richard III (*The True Tragedy*), Henry IV, and Henry V (both covered by *The Famous Victories of Henry V*), all subjects of plays by Shakespeare himself in the 1590s, as well as *King Leir* which, as well as being the major source for Shakespeare's *King Lear*, has possibly left its trace on a number of his earlier works. Though he was influenced by many other plays, not least the work of Christopher Marlowe, in developing his own style in his early works, there is no comparable body of sustained influence. If not actually in the Queen's Men, he certainly seems to have known their work especially well and the plays that belonged to them were crucial to Shakespeare's histories, the works that established the Lord Chamberlain's Men as the pre-eminent company of the age. The Queen's Men's works were virulently anti-Catholic and the company may even have owed its existence to a political aim of touring anti-Catholic propaganda; Shakespeare's plays that owe something of their existence to the Queen's Men's repertory, while hardly being Catholic apologetics, are strikingly less factional in their religion. . . .

Death of Hamnet and the Writing of Hamlet

On 11 August 1596 Hamnet Shakespeare was buried. It is too easy to assume that all expressions of grief in the plays thereafter were a reaction to his son's death, but something of Viola's passionate mourning for the apparent death of her twin brother in *Twelfth Night* could have been generated by the loss of Hamnet, Shakespeare's only male heir. It is not too fanciful to see Shakespeare drawn as a result towards the subject matter of *Hamlet*, where son grieves for father rather than father for son. . . .

Shakespeare wrote *Hamlet*, rewriting the 'Hamlet' play that had been playing on the London stage by 1589 and may have been written by Thomas Kyd. Now lost and probably never printed, the earlier play and its own sources can be presumed to have provided a similar narrative but a simpler one. Nothing in them would have been as complex or provocative as Shakespeare's creation of the prince whose thought processes have been so profoundly influential on Western literature. Whatever else made the writing of *Hamlet* happen at this time, the extraordinary talents of Richard Burbage were a major determinant on the creation of the role, his lifelike acting deeply affecting Shakespeare's portrayal of the prince's mind. But, in creating Ophelia, Shakespeare seems also to have remembered a Stratford event, the inquest into the drowning, just outside Stratford in December 1579, of the aptly named Katherine Hamlett.

The Death of a Son and a Father

G.B. Harrison

George Bagshawe Harrison (1894–1991) was a noted Shakespeare scholar, editor, and teacher. New Catholic Encyclopedia *is a reference work on Catholic history and belief intended as a reference for teachers, students, and other readers interested in practices, doctrine, and the history of the Catholic faith.*

The article discusses the early family life of William Shakespeare, including the baptism of his children and the death of his son Hamnet. According to the article, by 1598, two years after the death of his son, Shakespeare had established his reputation as a dramatist. It is believed that Shakespeare, along with his father, had Catholic leanings, especially based on the portrayal of Catholic characters in his plays. Particularly in Hamlet, *Catholic doctrine and sentiments are prevalent, while other plays paint Protestants in a negative light. Ultimately, the article states, Shakespeare's religious affiliation must remain unsolved, though it is believed that he died a papist.*

The facts of Shakespeare's life, preserved in authentic records, are considerable. Unfortunately he left no diaries or personal letters nor did he attract the notice of gossips or note takers, so that all attempts to write an intimate life must rely on guesswork.

On Nov. 28, 1582, a license was issued by the Bishop of Worcester to "William Shagspere" to marry "Anne Hathwey" of Stratford after one reading of the banns. According to the inscription on her gravestone, Anne Shakespeare died on Aug. 6, 1623, aged 67 years, and was thus eight years older than her husband. Their three children were baptized in Stratford church—Susanna on May 26, 1583, and Hamnet and Judith (twins) on Feb. 2, 1585. Nothing is certainly known of Shakespeare's early manhood; traditions that he was forced to flee Stratford for stealing deer from Sir Thomas Lucy, the local magnate, and that he was for some time a schoolmaster in the country are disputed and unverifiable but may have some foundation in fact.

Becoming a Playwright and Early Career

From 1592 onward the outline of Shakespeare's life is clear. He had become an actor and playwright in London. On March 3, 1592, Philip Henslowe, owner of the Rose playhouse, noted in his account book the first performance of "harey the vj" (presumably *1 Henry VI*), which was the most successful play of the season. Shakespeare was now attracting attention. In August he was venomously attacked by Robert Greene in *A Groatsworth of Wit* (published posthumously). His first poem, *Venus and Adonis,* was entered for printing on April 18, 1593, with a signed dedication to Henry Wriothesley, Earl of Southampton, to whom Shakespeare also dedicated *The Rape of Lucrece* in May 1594. By the end of the year he was a leading sharer in the Lord Chamberlain's company of players, and was mentioned with Richard Burbage and William Kempe as receiving payment for court performances during the Christmas holidays. Shakespeare's son Hamnet was buried Aug. 11, 1596. In October a grant of arms was issued by the College of Heralds to Shakespeare's father, whereby father and son were entitled to call themselves gentlemen. On May 4, 1597, Shakespeare was able to purchase for #60 a large house known as New Place in the center of Stratford. By 1598, Shakespeare's reputation as a dramatist was established. In September 1598, Shakespeare acted a part in Jonson's *Every Man in His Humor*. At the end of the year he, with six other members of the Chamberlain's Company, shared in the expense of erecting the new Globe playhouse on the bankside. On May 1, 1602, he bought 107 acres of arable land in Stratford for #320.

Queen Elizabeth I died on March 24, 1603. Her successor, James I, soon after arriving in London, appointed the Chamberlain's Company to be his own players—The King's Men, as they were henceforward known—and in the license of appointment, Shakespeare's name stands second. Thereafter the King's Men prospered; in the new reign they acted at court four times as often as under the old Queen.

William Shakespeare was born at Stratford-on-Avon, married at 18, and after a manhood spent no one knows how and where, became a successful dramatist in London; that he prospered and invested his gains; that he died and was buried in his native town (to the great profit of subsequent inhabitants). The lack of heroic or romantic anecdotes has proved so disappointing to some that they have even denied that William Shakespeare of Stratford was indeed the author of his own plays—a doubt which no reputable scholar has ever endorsed.

The Art of Drama

Hamlet, the most fascinating and most controverted play ever written, and *Othello*, the best constructed of all the tragedies, were written at the turn of the century, as was *Troilus and Cressida*, a bitter comment on false and romantic notions of love, honor, and war. The art of drama had advanced very rapidly in the last years of the old queen, and Shakespeare now had rivals, chief among them Jonson, Marston, Chapman and Dekker. Playgoers had become keen, critical, and sophisticated in their demands. At the accession of James I in March 1603, the prospects of Shakespeare's company improved, especially after the king had made them his own players; but in May the worst outbreak of plague for many years again interrupted play going until the end of the year.

Actor Christopher Eccleston is shown portraying Hamlet as he contemplates life and death in the famous soliloquy that begins, "To be, or not to be." Some hypothesize that the intense grief in Hamlet *was a result of Shakespeare suffering through the death of his son, Hamnet.* © Donald Cooper/Photostage.

Catholicism in Shakespeare's Life

Shakespeare has been claimed by Catholics, Anglicans, Puritans, and agnostics. For the Anglican claim, it can be pointed out that he and his children were all baptized in the Anglican church at Stratford, in which he was also buried. In his plays he echoes the English Bible and the Anglican Book of Common Prayer. But he shows equally a considerable knowledge of Catholic teaching, doctrine, and practice; and there is good evidence that his father, John Shakespeare, was a zealous Catholic, for in 1592 his name appears in a list of 42 who were reported to the Bishop of Worcester as "recusants."

More significant is a little-known document called "John Shakespeare's Will." The original, long since destroyed, was found hidden in the tiles of his house in Henley Street at Stratford. A transcript was made by a local antiquary, John Jordan, and published in *The Gentleman's Magazine* in 1783. The document was accepted as genuine by Edmund Malone, who reprinted it in his edition of Shakespeare's works in 1790. The will is a profession of the Catholic faith in the form of a spiritual testament in 14 clauses, each beginning with "I, John Shakespeare." The testator declares that at the time of writing he may die unprepared by any sacrament, and if so he prays that he may be spiritually anointed. This form of spiritual testament was drawn up by St. Charles BORROMEO and was especially designed for times of religious persecution. Versions are known in Spanish, Italian, and the Swiss dialect. It is a sign of John Shakespeare's steadfastness that he hid rather than burnt so dangerous a document, especially after the troubles that befell his wife's family in 1583–84.

The senior member of the Arden family at that time was Edward Arden of Park Hall, who maintained a priest, Hugh Hall, to say Mass. In 1583, when the mission of St. Edmund CAMPION was still disturbing the Privy Council, Edward Arden's son-in-law. John Somerville, oppressed by private and religious troubles, went out of his mind, eluded his family, and made for London where he was heard to utter wild threats against the life of Elizabeth. As a result the whole family was involved in a charge of high treason. Edward Arden was condemned to death and executed by quartering at Smithfield on Dec. 26, 1584. His wife and Hall were also condemned. Mrs. Arden was subsequently pardoned; the priest and Somerville died in prison. Edward Arden was a cousin of Shakespeare's mother. Shakespeare was 20 at this time. In Warwickshire the chief agent in the persecution of the Ardens was that Sir Thomas Lucy who, according to the legends of Shakespeare's early manhood, was the cause of his flight from Stratford. When Shakespeare reemerged from obscurity, he dedicated his *Venus and Adonis* to the young Earl of Southampton, whose family was Catholic.

Question of Religious Affiliation

It is thus likely that Shakespeare was brought up in a Catholic home, but there is no evidence that he practiced the faith in his maturity. His sympathies in the plays—so far as the plays can be used as evidence—are generally Catholic. His priests, such as Friar Laurence in *Romeo and Juliet,* Friar Francis in *Much Ado,* the priest in *Twelfth Night,* are grave, patient, well-meaning men whom everyone respects. In *Measure for Measure,* the Duke, for worthy motives, disguises himself as a friar, and even hears confessions—an action which no one seemed to question.

The few Protestant ministers who appear in the plays are less admirable. Sir Hugh Evans in *The Merry Wives* is amusing; Sir Nathaniel in *Love's Labour's Lost* is a worthy man and a good bowler though an indifferent actor; in *As You Like It,* Sir Oliver Martext is a poor specimen. It is also relevant that in his version of *King John,* Shakespeare wiped out the hearty anti-Catholic propaganda of the old play he recast. In *Hamlet* there are several instances of Catholic doctrine and sentiment. The Ghost of Hamlet's father, for example, comes back from Purgatory (and not, as was more usual with returned ghosts in Elizabethan dramas, from a classical Hades), whither he was suddenly dispatched "unhouseled, disappointed, unanealed"—without absolution, preparation or Extreme Unction; but to Hamlet, death is a consummation devoutly to be wished only if it leads to the annihilation of a dreamless sleep. Hamlet himself is more interested in man than in God.

While the early plays are sprinkled with Christian sentiments, orthodox and often quite conventional, the later plays, especially the tragedies, seem to indicate that Shakespeare had lapsed into an almost Greek belief in fate.

Until further evidence is available, the question of Shakespeare's religious convictions and practice must remain unsolved. There is no record that he ever suffered for his faith either in purse or in person; unlike his father or Ben Jonson, he is not known to have been delated as a recusant or fined for failure to attend the services of the state Church. Nevertheless there is the flat statement of Archdeacon Richard Davies (d. 1708), a Warwickshire antiquary, that "he died a papist."

The Issue of Corruption
in *Hamlet*

Corruption in Denmark

A.C. Bradley

A.C. Bradley (1851–1935), a leading Shakespearean scholar of the late nineteenth and early twentieth centuries, ended his teaching career as a professor at Oxford University.

In the following selection, Bradley concentrates on Hamlet's melancholy which has been generated by the corrupt kingdom, king, queen, and court. At one time, Hamlet was decisive and heroic, but his encounter with the Ghost of his father is the turning point. Learning that his uncle killed Hamlet's father, took over the kingdom which was Hamlet's inheritance, and married his "faithless" mother (which some believed to be an act of incest) makes Hamlet profoundly despondent. With what he believes to be clear evidence of the Ghost's charges during the play and with Claudius at prayer, Hamlet's actions become tainted. With increased cynicism in this atmosphere of corruption, he sends his old college friends to their deaths, kills Polonius, destroys both Ophelia and Laertes, and sends the remaining characters and himself to death. In conclusion, Bradley sees one factor not open to character analysis: the hand of God working throughout the play.

Hamlet, at the close of the First Act, . . . had just received his charge from the spirit of his father; and his condition was vividly depicted in the fact that, within an hour of receiving this charge, he had relapsed into that weariness of life or longing for death which is the immediate cause of his later inaction. When next we meet him, at the opening of the Second

A.C. Bradley, *Shakesperean Tragedy: Lectures on Hamlet, Othello, King Lear, Macbeth.* Basingstoke, Hampshire: MacMillan and Co. Ltd., 1956. First edition, 1904. Second edition, March 1905, reprinted August 1905, 1906, 1908, 1910, 1911, 1912, 1914, 1915, 1916, 1918, 1919, 1920 (twice), 1922, 1924, 1926, 1929, 1932, 1937, 1941, 1949, 1950, 1951, 1952, 1956. All rights reserved. Reproduced with permission of Palgrave Macmillan.

Act, a considerable time has elapsed, apparently as much as two months. The ambassadors sent to the King of Norway are just returning. Laertes, whom we saw leaving Elsinore, has been in Paris long enough to be in want of fresh supplies. Ophelia has obeyed her father's command, and has refused to receive Hamlet's visits or letters.

Corruption Brings on Melancholy

What has Hamlet done? He has put on an 'antic disposition' and established a reputation for lunacy, with the result that his mother has become deeply anxious about him, and with the further result that the King, who was formerly so entirely at ease regarding him that he wished him to stay on at Court, is now extremely uneasy and very desirous to discover the cause of his 'transformation.' Hence Rosencrantz and Guildenstern have been sent for, to cheer him by their company and to worm his secret out of him; and they are just about to arrive. Beyond exciting thus the apprehensions of his enemy Hamlet has done absolutely nothing; and, as we have seen, we must imagine him during this long period sunk for the most part in 'bestial oblivion' or fruitless broodings, and falling deeper and deeper into the slough of despond. . . .

Finding out the Truth

The King is satisfied that, whatever else may be the hidden cause of Hamlet's madness, it is not love. He is by no means certain even that Hamlet is mad at all. He has heard that infuriated threat, 'I say, we will have no more marriages; those that are married, all but one, shall live; the rest shall keep as they are.' He is thoroughly alarmed. He at any rate will not delay. On the spot he determines to send Hamlet to England. But, as Polonius is present, we do not learn at once the meaning of this purpose.

Evening comes. The approach of the play-scene raises Hamlet's spirits. . . . He is in his element. He feels that he is doing *something* towards his end, striking a stroke, but a stroke of intellect. In his instructions to the actor on the delivery of the inserted speech, and again in his conversation with Horatio just before the entry of the Court, we see the true Hamlet, the Hamlet of the days before his father's death. But how characteristic it is that he appears quite as anxious that his speech should not be ranted as that Horatio should observe its effect upon the King! This trait appears again even at that thrilling moment when the actor is just going to deliver the speech. Hamlet sees him beginning to frown and glare like the conventional stage-murderer, and calls to him impatiently, 'Leave thy damnable faces and begin!'

Hamlet's device proves a triumph far more complete than he had dared to expect. He had thought the King might 'blench,' but he does much more. When only six of the 'dozen or sixteen lines' have been spoken he starts to his feet and rushes from the hall, followed by the whole dismayed Court. In the elation of success—an elation at first almost hysterical—Hamlet treats Rosencrantz and Guildenstern, who are sent to him, with undisguised contempt.

In this mood, on his way to his mother's chamber, he comes upon the King, alone, kneeling, conscience-stricken and attempting to pray. His enemy is delivered into his hands.

> Now might I do it pat, now he is praying:
>
> And now I'll do it: and so he goes to heaven:
>
> And so am I revenged. That would be scanned.

He scans it; and the sword that he drew at the words, 'And now I'll do it,' is thrust back into its sheath. If he killed the villain now he would send his soul to heaven; and he would fain kill soul as well as body. . . .

Turning-Point of the Tragedy

Shakespeare has taken care to give this perfect opportunity so repulsive a character that we can hardly bring ourselves to wish that the hero should accept it. One of his minor difficulties, we have seen, probably was that he seemed to be required to attack a defenceless man; and here this difficulty is at its maximum.

This incident is, again, the turning-point of the tragedy. So far, Hamlet's delay, though it is endangering his freedom and his life, has done no irreparable harm; but his failure here is the cause of all the disasters that follow. In sparing the King, he sacrifices Polonius, Ophelia, Rosencrantz and Guildenstern, Laertes, the Queen and himself. This central significance of the passage is dramatically indicated in the following scene by the reappearance of the Ghost and the repetition of its charge.

Polonius is the first to fall.

Polonius Is a Cause and Victim of Corruption

When, then, at the opening of the interview between Hamlet and his mother, the son, instead of listening to her remonstrances, roughly assumes the offensive, she becomes alarmed; and when, on her attempting to leave the room, he takes her by the arm and forces her to sit down, she is terrified, cries out, 'Thou wilt not murder me?' and screams for help. Polonius, behind the arras, echoes her call; and in a moment Hamlet, hoping the concealed person is the King, runs the old man through the body.

Evidently this act is intended to stand in sharp contrast with Hamlet's sparing of his enemy. The King would have been just as defenceless behind the arras as he had been on his knees; but here Hamlet is already excited and in action, and the chance comes to him so suddenly that he has no time to 'scan' it. It is a minor consideration, but still for the dramatist not unimportant, that the audience would wholly sympathise with Hamlet's attempt here, as directed against an enemy who is lurking to entrap him, instead of being engaged in a

Hamlet has inspired many remakes and revivals, such as this 1999 film staring Ethan Hawke as Hamlet, Diane Venora as Gertrude, and Kyle McLachlan as Claudius. In the role, Hawke explores Hamlet's melancholy, which has been generated by the corrupt individuals around him. Miramax/The Kobal Collection/The Picture Desk, Inc.

business which perhaps to the bulk of the audience then, as now, seemed to have a 'relish of salvation in't.' . . .

Leaving Reluctantly

It appears that Hamlet has somehow learned of the King's design of sending him to England in charge of his two 'schoolfellows.' He has no doubt that this design covers some villainous plot against himself, but neither does he doubt that he will succeed in defeating it; . . . he looks forward with pleasure to this conflict of wits. The idea of refusing to go appears not to occur to him. Perhaps (for here we are left to conjecture) he feels that he could not refuse unless at the same time he openly accused the King of his father's murder (a course which he seems at no time to contemplate); for by the slaughter of Polonius he has supplied his enemy with the best possible excuse for getting him out of the country. Besides, he has so effectually warned this enemy that, after the death of Polonius is discovered, he is kept under guard. He consents, then, to go.

But on his way to the shore he meets the army of Fortinbras on its march to Poland; and the sight of these men going cheerfully to risk death 'for an egg-shell,' and 'making mouths at the invisible event,' strikes him with shame as he remembers how he, with so much greater cause for action, 'lets all sleep;' and he breaks out into the soliloquy, 'How all occasions do inform against me!' . . .

The Destruction of Ophelia and Laertes

When the action recommences, the death of Polonius has led to the insanity of Ophelia and the secret return of Laertes from France. The young man comes back breathing slaughter. For the King, afraid to put Hamlet on his trial (a course likely to raise the question of his own behaviour at the play, and perhaps to provoke an open accusation), has attempted to hush up the circumstances of Polonius's death, and has given him a hurried and inglorious burial. The fury of Laertes, therefore, is directed in the first instance against the King: and the ease with which he raises the people, like the King's fear of a judicial enquiry, shows us how purely internal were the obstacles which the hero had to overcome. This impression is intensified by the broad contrast between Hamlet and Laertes, who rushes headlong to his revenge, and is determined to have it though allegiance, conscience, grace and damnation stand in his way. But the King, though he has been hard put to it, is now in his element and feels safe. Knowing that he will very soon hear of Hamlet's execution in England, he tells Laertes that his father died by Hamlet's hand, and expresses his willingness to let the friends of Laertes judge whether he himself has any responsibility for the deed. And when, to his astonishment and dismay, news comes that Hamlet has returned to Denmark, he acts with admirable promptitude and address, turns Laertes round his finger, and arranges with him for the murder of their common enemy. . . .

Friends and Sanity

Hamlet's return to Denmark is due partly to his own action, partly to accident. On the voyage he secretly possesses himself of the royal commission, and substitutes for it another, which he himself writes and seals, and in which the King of England is ordered to put to death, not Hamlet, but Rosencrantz and Guildenstern. . . .

I incline to think that Shakespeare means to show in the Hamlet of the Fifth Act a slight thinning of the dark cloud of melancholy, and means us to feel it tragic that this change comes too late. . . .

Claudius the Corruptor

King Claudius rarely gets from the reader the attention he deserves. . . .

He is no tragic character. He had a small nature. If Hamlet may be trusted, he was a man of mean appearance—a mildewed ear, a toad, a bat; and he was also bloated by excess in drinking. People made mouths at him in contempt while his brother lived; and though, when he came to the throne, they spent large sums in buying his portrait, he evidently put little reliance on their loyalty. He was no villain of force, who thought of winning his brother's crown by a bold and open stroke, but a cut-purse who stole the diadem from a shelf and put it in his pocket. He had the inclination of natures physically weak and morally small towards intrigue and crooked dealing. His instinctive predilection was for poison: this was the means he used in his first murder, and he at once recurred to it when he had failed to get Hamlet executed by deputy. Though in danger he showed no cowardice, his first thought was always for himself. . . .

The Hand of Providence

As *Hamlet* nears its close the 'religious' tone of the tragedy is deepened in two ways. In the first place, 'accident' is introduced into the plot in its barest and least dramatic form; when Hamlet is brought back to Denmark by the chance of the meeting with the pirate ship. This incident has been therefore severely criticised as a lame expedient, but it appears probable that the 'accident' is meant to impress the imagination as the very reverse of accidental, and with many readers it certainly does so. And that this was the intention is made the more likely by a second fact, the fact that in connection with the events of the voyage Shakespeare introduces that feeling, on Hamlet's part, of his being in the hands of Providence. The repeated expressions of this feeling are not, I have maintained, a sign that Hamlet has now formed a fixed resolution to do his duty forthwith; but their effect is to strengthen in the spectator the feeling that, whatever may become of Hamlet, and whether he wills it or not, his task will surely be accomplished, because it is the purpose of a power against which both he and his enemy are impotent, and which makes of them the instruments of its own will.

The Ghost as Messenger of Divine Justice

Observing this, we may remember another significant point of resemblance between *Hamlet* and *Macbeth*, the appearance in each play of a Ghost,—a figure which seems quite in place in either, whereas it would seem utterly out of place in *Othello* or *King Lear*. Much might be said of the Ghost in *Hamlet*, but I confine myself to the matter which we are now considering. What is the effect of the appearance of the Ghost? And, in particular, why does Shakespeare make this Ghost so *majestical* a phantom, giving it that measured and solemn utterance, and that air of impersonal abstraction which forbids, for example, all expression of affection for Hamlet and checks in Hamlet the outburst of pity for his father? Whatever the intention may have been, the result is that the Ghost affects imagination not simply as the apparition of a dead king who desires the accomplishment of *his* purposes, but also as the representative of that hidden ultimate power, the messenger of divine justice set upon the expiation of offences which it appeared impossible for man to discover and avenge, a reminder or a symbol of the connection of the limited world of ordinary experience with the vaster life of which it is but a partial appearance. And as, at the beginning of the play, we have this intimation, conveyed through the medium of the received religious idea of a soul come from purgatory, so at the end, conveyed through the similar idea of a soul carried by angels to its rest, we have an intimation of the same character, and a reminder that the apparent failure of Hamlet's life is not the ultimate truth concerning him.

If these various peculiarities of the tragedy are considered, it will be agreed that, while *Hamlet* certainly cannot be called in the specific sense a 'religious drama,' there is in it nevertheless both a freer use of popular religious ideas, and a more decided, though always imaginative, intimation of a supreme power concerned in human evil and good, than can be found in any other of Shakespeare's tragedies. And this is probably one of the causes of the special popularity of this play, just as *Macbeth*, the tragedy which in these respects most nearly approaches it, has also the place next to it in general esteem.

Politics in *Hamlet*

John Erskine Hankins

John Erskine Hankins, who died in 1996, was a prolific writer on Shakespeare. His teaching career included a position as chair of the English Department at the University of Maine.

Hankins in the following selection posits a parallel relationship between historical events in England and Denmark and discusses questions of morality, religion, and statecraft relevant to each. Citing problems of the Tudor monarchy, particularly the question of the rightful accession to the throne, compared with Claudius's rise to kingship, Hankins notes that both countries used a limited "elective" system. An Elizabethan would have seen the parallels between Claudius's marriage to Gertrude (partially done to politically stabilize Denmark) and Henry VIII's marriage to the widow of his dead brother, Arthur. Additionally, Hankins notes that the differing Catholic and Protestant views of the legitimacy of such marriages were major factors in history and in Hamlet. *The divine right of kings helps explain the differences between Hamlet's view of Claudius and the attitude held by Rosencrantz, Guildenstern, and Horatio. These parallels would have been clear to Elizabethan audiences, Hankins contends.*

I believe that contemporary ideas of politics and religion are evident in *Hamlet,* that to some extent they reflect actual situations and controversies of Shakespeare's time, and that the play was thus more intelligible to his age than it is to ours. . . .

An English Political Context

Though the scene of *Hamlet* is medieval Denmark, most critics will agree that its characters and problems are those of sixteenth-century England. As is his usual custom, Shakespeare writes of his own day, regardless of where and when the action of his drama takes place. This is truer of *Hamlet* than has been generally supposed.

An apparent difference between Hamlet's Denmark and Shakespeare's England is that the former was an elective monarchy. This conclusion is based on Hamlet's use of the word "election" in referring to the manner of choosing the Danish king. A glance at a Shakespearean concordance, however, will show that "election" simply means "choice" (Lat. *electio*), whether by a group or by an individual; Hamlet himself uses it once in referring to an individual choice. Thus, while it is obvious that the Danish king was chosen by some group, we need not think of his choice in terms of a modern general election. Who the electors were is indicated by Fortinbras at the end of the play. Seizing the opportunity to assert his own claims to the throne, he bids Horatio "call the noblest to the audience", a line which indicates that the kingdom's affairs were handled by a council of nobles or others of high rank.

Now this situation was not very different from that in England and in Scotland during the sixteenth century. Normally, succession to the throne went by the rule of primogeniture [firstborn], but so confused were the claims of Henry VIII's two daughters that an Act of Parliament was necessary to establish the order of succession. In Scotland the Lords took the responsibility of forcing Mary Stuart's abdication and appointing her son James to the throne. Thus, in the sixteenth century several British sovereigns were chosen by much the same kind of "election" that we find in *Hamlet*.

England's anxiety over the succession to the throne is further indicated in this play. The last act of Hamlet's life is to name his choice of a successor:

But I do prophesy th' election lights

On Fortinbras: he has my dying voice.

Since Hamlet himself had been formally named as Claudius' successor, after Claudius' death it is Hamlet's duty to name his own choice of a successor. The implication seems to be that the sovereign's word carried great weight but was not necessarily decisive in such a case. . . .

The Political Crisis in Denmark

It is clear at the beginning of *Hamlet* that Denmark is facing a national crisis. She is arming at a feverish pace in preparation for war. The reasons are fully explained. Fortinbras of Norway has demanded the return of territories lost by his father and is threatening invasion of Denmark. He has taken advantage of the confusion attendant upon a change of government to press his claims, and it is reasonable to suppose that he presented them as soon as he learned of the elder Hamlet's death. The state needed a head, and quickly. Hamlet had been out of the country and, whether or not he had returned before the election, was probably less experienced in statecraft than Claudius. How natural, then, that the country should turn in a dire emergency to the elder prince already in charge of affairs, especially as this meant only a postponement of Hamlet's ascent to the throne. So it must have appeared to the Danish public. As a matter of fact, Claudius justified their confidence. His appeal to the King of Norway to intervene was successful, and Denmark was saved from a ruinous war.

It also seems likely that the quick marriage of Claudius and Gertrude was presented to the public as a result of this same crisis. In his first appearance upon the stage, at a formal assembly of his court, the King announces his marriage to Gertrude and explains that the exigencies of the time have required it. It is more fitting that they should be mourning his brother's death;

Yet so far hath discretion fought with nature

That we with wisest sorrow think on him,

Together with remembrance of ourselves.

This is a clear statement that the marriage has been contracted as a matter of public policy. A moment later the King says:

Nor have we herein barr'd

Your better wisdoms, which have freely gone

With this affair along.

Thus the marriage was undertaken with the advice and approval of his council, its quickness being probably justified by the necessity of consolidating all factions within the kingdom to face a national emergency. From the announcement of his marriage Claudius turns immediately to a discussion of the emergency, a proximity of subject matter which is perhaps significant.

Political Marriages in Denmark and England

An Elizabethan audience would quickly see the political value of such a marriage. It would satisfy the adherents of the Queen, "imperial jointress" of Denmark, who would retain her former rank. It would satisfy the adherents of Hamlet, since it would insure his succession to the throne; any sons born to Claudius would be Hamlet's younger brothers and therefore not serious rivals. The King has this in mind when he formally proclaims Hamlet "the most immediate to our throne" and accepts him as his own son. Hamlet is to be officially his "son" and therefore heir to the throne. To the public this must have seemed a fair arrangement; it may even have been part of the agreement by which Claudius was elected

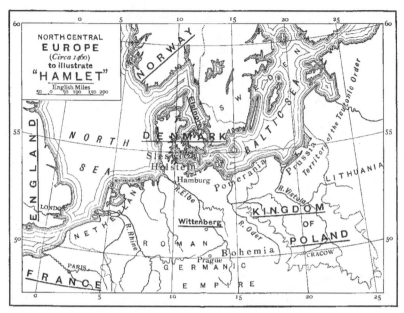

This line drawing from The Works of William Shakespeare *illustrates the location of* Hamlet *with a map of Denmark and Europe. The politics that permeate the play were inspired by historical events in England at the time.*

king. Hence Rosencrantz expresses genuine surprise at Hamlet's resentment "when you have the voice of the king himself for your succession in Denmark". It is an ironic feature of Hamlet's position that the marriage which so shocks him is ostensibly for the purpose of safeguarding his own rights. Its political explanation is further strengthened by the absence of any embarrassment on the part of Claudius and Gertrude. Whatever their real motives, the world sees their marriage as a matter of public policy and patriotic duty; if inclination should agree with duty, so much the better.

The marriage of relatives to unite rival claims to the throne is not uncommon in British history. Mary Queen of Scots married her first cousin Darnley to strengthen her position in this manner. Richard III attempted to marry his niece Elizabeth in order to strengthen his position, but she escaped him and married Henry VII, uniting the rival houses of York and Lancaster. Still, it may be questioned whether British opinion would have sanctioned such a union as that of Claudius and Gertrude, since this involved marriage to a brother's widow, forbidden in both the Roman and the Anglican churches. Hamlet himself does not like it and calls the marriage incestuous; the union of his "uncle-father and aunt-mother" fills him with disgust. But how would the Elizabethan public have regarded it?

The answer is that such a marriage, justified by political reasons, did take place and changed the course of English history: the marriage of Henry VIII to Katherine of Aragon. It is the most important element of Shakespeare's play *Henry VIII*. Furthermore, though Henry had been dead over fifty years when *Hamlet* was written, his first marriage was still a live political issue, since it involved Elizabeth's right to occupy the English throne.

It will be remembered that Henry VII's eldest son Arthur was married to Katherine of Aragon to cement an alliance between England and Spain. When Arthur died before his father, it was decided to preserve the alliance by wedding Katherine to Arthur's brother Henry. . . . A special dispensation from the Pope was secured, and the marriage took place. After some twenty years, during which Katherine brought him one daughter, Mary, but no living sons, Henry affected to believe his lack of a male heir a divine punishment for his "incestuous" marriage and applied to the Church for a divorce, which the Pope refused to grant. This disagreement, together with the English clergy's discontent at Italian domination, caused an open break with Rome and the establishment of the Anglican Church. To Henry's second wife, Anne Boleyn, was born Elizabeth; to his third, Jane Seymour, was born Edward. The first of these children was born while Katherine was still alive and, in Catholic eyes, still the wife of Henry VIII.

Religion and Marriage

For three-quarters of a century marriage to a brother's widow became a political as well as a moral issue. True Catholics considered Henry's divorce illegal and his younger daughter illegitimate. Marriage to a brother's widow was justified *when urgently required as a matter of state*, since this consideration had persuaded the Pope to allow it. The order of succession after Henry should be: Edward; Mary Tudor; Mary Stuart, Queen of Scots, daughter of Henry's sister; Mary's son, James VI of Scotland.

The Protestants took a different view. Marriage to a brother's widow was incestuous and not even the Pope's dispensation could hallow it; hence Henry's divorce was legal, and Mary Tudor's legitimacy was at least doubtful, since she was born of an incestuous union. . . .

Something of this conflict between political and moral considerations is reflected in *Hamlet*. Was Claudius' marriage to Gertrude incestuous and unlawful, even though urgently required as a matter of state? English Protestants would have answered yes; English Catholics, no. Hamlet expresses the Protestant viewpoint; the council which acquiesced in the marriage represents the Catholic attitude. . . .

Plots and Murders

Hamlet's hesitancy in killing Claudius has a parallel in Elizabeth's hesitancy to execute Mary Stuart. From the time of Mary's flight to England, she was a constant source of danger to the throne. Long before Mary's death, Elizabeth's advisers urged that she be killed and the danger removed. . . . The danger could easily be removed by Mary's death, since the Catholics had no particular wish to hasten James' ascent of the throne. Yet, despite the urgent remonstrance of her advisers, Elizabeth delayed this obvious solution for many years, during which her own life was in mortal danger. . . .

It is apparent here that Elizabeth faced a problem much like that of Hamlet and answered it in the same way. She knew that Mary was plotting against her and was a source of danger, but that Mary actually sought her life she was not sure. She could have ended the suspense by "action," as her most astute advisers urged her to do; like Laertes, she could have taken vengeance on one who caused her an injury, whether the injury was intended or not. Instead she delayed while her people, like modern critics of Hamlet, considered such delay the height of reprehensible folly. . . .

The Divine Right of Kings

The theory of Divine Right is based upon an ideal of kingship which has much in common with the "leader" concept in German political thought of today [in 1941]. The king is the heaven-ordained instrument of the people's will, and through him they are able to act. Hence his person is sacred since in him is bound up the welfare of a whole people. . . .

Since the king, as it were, incarnates the state in his own person, it follows that regicide [the killing of a king] is an enterprise of the gravest import, not to be lightly undertaken or accomplished. The king is God's vicegerent in temporal affairs, and to kill him an unholy act. . . .

It seems to me that there is a difference in the attitudes of Horatio and Hamlet on this point, though the clues indicating it are very slight. Horatio judges sovereigns as kings, his superiors, while Hamlet judges them as men, his equals. When Horatio says of Hamlet's father, "I saw him once; he was a goodly *king*," Hamlet replies:

He was a *man*, take him for all in all,

I shall not look upon his like again.

And when Horatio finally condemns Claudius, he exclaims, "Why, what a *king* is this!" Perhaps his earlier reticence was in part due to the feeling that an "inferior subject" should not presume to pass judgment on the conduct of sovereigns. Hamlet, on the other hand, has no such scruples. As one who is kingly in rank and the rightful heir of Denmark's crown, he can properly judge Claudius and punish him. . . .

The Elizabethan View

To assume that the whole play of *Hamlet* is an elaborate historical allegory is a mistake, as the various elements of the plot cannot be made to coincide perfectly with any particular sequence of events. But in its use of problems and specific situations of contemporary politics, the play must have appeared to Elizabethans as a commentary on their age. I have shown several situations in which Hamlet faced the same problems as Queen Elizabeth. In the matter of marriage, in the question of whether to kill a rival for the throne who was suspected of seeking his life, in the detection of an incriminating letter, in nominating his successor as the last act of his life—in all these respects Hamlet's experience closely parallels that of Elizabeth. . . . To an audience viewing *Hamlet* shortly after her death, the political element of the play would have been quite clear.

Sickness in Denmark

Caroline F.E. Spurgeon

Caroline F.E. Spurgeon (1869–1942) was an English literary critic and professor at Bedford College in England. Although she is chiefly known for her Shakespeare studies, she is also the author of 500 Years of Chaucer.

Spurgeon finds certain images flowing through William Shakespeare's plays much as one might discover a motif in music or a theme in a work of art, thus giving a clear idea of the way Shakespeare looked at the play and a conception of its dominant idea. In Hamlet, images of sickness and bodily disfigurations project a sense of decay that pervades the entire kingdom, like a tumor, eating away at one's being. This describes the spiritual and moral factors of the state of Denmark. These are not mere images of personal anguish, but rather projections of rottenness, corruption, and total decay. As for Hamlet, his problem is not one of will, reasoning, philosophy, or temperament. He too is the victim of a pervasive condition, and he is no more responsible for what he does than is, in Spurgeon's words, a "sick man to blame for the cancer which devours him."

It has not, so far as I know, ever yet been noticed that recurrent images play a part in raising, developing, sustaining and repeating emotion in the tragedies, which is somewhat analogous to the action of a recurrent theme or 'motif' in a musical fugue or sonata, or in one of Wagner's operas. . . .

Dominating Images

These dominating images are a characteristic of Shakespeare's work throughout, but whereas in the earlier plays they are often rather obvious and of set design, taken over in some cases with the story itself from a hint in the original narrative; in the later plays, and especially in the great tragedies, they are born of the emotions of the theme and are, as in *Macbeth*, subtle, complex, varied, but intensely vivid and revealing; or as in *Lear*, so constant and all-pervading as to be reiterated, not only in the word pictures, but also in the single words themselves. . . .

I found that there is a certain range of images, and roughly a certain proportion of these, to be expected in every play, and that certain familiar categories, of Nature, animals, and what one may call 'everyday' or 'domestic,' easily come first. But in addition to this normal grouping, I have found, especially in the tragedies, certain groups of images which, as it were, stick out in each particular play and immediately attract attention because they are peculiar either in subject, or quantity, or both.

These seem to form the floating image or images in Shakespeare's mind called forth by that particular play, and I propose now, as briefly as possible, just to look at the tragedies from the point of view of these groups of images only. . . .

Sickness and Poison Equal Corruption

In *Hamlet*, . . . if we look closely we see . . . images of sickness, disease or blemish of the body, in the play, and we discover that the idea of an ulcer or tumour, as descriptive of the unwholesome condition of Denmark morally, is, on the whole, the dominating one.

Hamlet speaks of his mother's sin as a blister on the 'fair forehead of an innocent love,' and the emotion is so strong and the picture so vivid, that the metaphor overflows into the verbs and adjectives; heaven's face, he tells her, is *thought-sick* at the act; her husband is a *mildew'd ear, blasting* his *wholesome* brother, and to have married him, her sense must be not only *sickly*, but *apoplex'd*, and at the end of that terrific scene he implores her not to soothe herself with the belief that his father's apparition is due to her son's madness, and not to her own guilt, for that

will but skin and film the ulcerous place,

Whiles rank corruption, mining all within,

Infects unseen.

So also, later, he compares the unnecessary fighting between Norway and Poland to a kind of tumour which grows out of too much prosperity. He sees the country and the people in it alike in terms of a sick body needing medicine or the surgeon's knife. When he surprises Claudius at his prayers, he exclaims

This physic but prolongs thy sickly days,

and he describes the action of conscience in the unforgettable picture of the healthy, ruddy countenance turning pale with sickness. A mote in the eye, a 'vicious mole', a galled chilblain, a probed wound and purgation, are also among Hamlet's images; and the mind of Claudius runs equally on the same theme.

When he hears of the murder of Polonius, he declares their weakness in not sooner having had Hamlet shut up was comparable to the cowardly action of a man with a 'foul disease' who

To keep it from divulging, let it feed

Even on the pith of life;

and later, when arranging to send Hamlet to England and to his death, he justifies it by the proverbial tag

diseases desperate grown

By desperate appliance are relieved,

Or not at all;

and adjures the English king to carry out his behest, in the words of a fever patient seeking a sedative,

For like the hectic in my blood he rages,

And thou must cure me.

When working on Laertes, so that he will easily fall in with the design for the fencing match, his speech is full of the same underlying thought of a body sick, or ill at ease,

goodness, growing to a plurisy,

Dies in his own too much,

and finally, he sums up the essence of the position and its urgency with lightning vividness in a short medical phrase,

But, to the quick o' the ulcer:

Hamlet comes back.

. . . Though bodily disease is emphasised, bodily action and strain are little drawn upon; indeed, only in Hamlet's great speech is it brought before us at all (*to be shot at* with slings and arrows, *to take arms against* troubles and *oppose* them, *to suffer* shocks, *to bear* the lash of whips, and *endure* pangs, to *grunt* and *sweat* under burdens, and so on), and here . . . it serves to intensify the feeling of mental anguish. In *Hamlet* . . . anguish is not the dominating thought, but *rottenness*, disease, corruption, the result of *dirt*; the people are 'muddied,'

Thick and unwholesome in their thoughts and whispers,

and this corruption is, in the words of Claudius, 'rank' and 'smells to heaven,' so that the state of things in Denmark which shocks, paralyses and finally overwhelms Hamlet, is as the foul tumour breaking inwardly and poisoning the whole body, while showing

no cause without

Why the man dies.

Thus, to Shakespeare's pictorial imagination, the problem in Hamlet is not predominantly that of will and reason, of a mind too philosophic or a nature temperamentally unfitted to act quickly; (he sees it pictorially,) *not as the problem of an individual at all,* but as something greater and even more mysterious, as a *condition* for which the individual himself is apparently not responsible, any more than the sick man is to blame for the cancer which strikes and devours him, but which, nevertheless, in its course and development, impartially and relentlessly, annihilates him and others, innocent and guilty alike. That is the tragedy of Hamlet, as it is perhaps the chief tragic mystery of life.

It is hardly necessary to point out, in a play so well known, and of such rich imaginative quality, how the ugliness of the dominating image (disease, ulcer) is counteracted, and the whole lighted up by flashes of sheer beauty in the imagery; beauty of picture, of sound and association, more particularly in the classical group and in the personifications. Thus, the tragic, murky atmosphere of Hamlet's interview with his mother, with its ever-repeated insistence on physical sickness and revolting disease, is illumined by the glow of his description of his father's portrait, the associations of beauty called up by Hyperion, Jove and Mars, or the exquisite picture evoked by the contemplation of the grace of his father's poise,

like the herald Mercury

New-lighted on a heaven-kissing hill.

These beauties are specially noticeable in the many personifications, as when, with Horatio, we see 'the morn in russet mantle clad,' as she 'walks o'er the dew of yon high eastward hill,' or with Hamlet, watch Laertes leaping into Ophelia's grave, and ask

> whose phrase of sorrow
>
> Conjures the wandering stars and makes them stand
>
> Like wonder-wounded hearers?

Peace, with her wheaten garland, Niobe all tears, Ophelia's garments 'heavy with their drink,' who pull her from her 'melodious lay' to muddy death, or the magnificent picture of the two sides of the Queen's nature at war, as seen by the elder Hamlet,

> But look, amazement on thy mother sits;
>
> O, step between her and her fighting soul:

these, and many more, are the unforgettable and radiant touches of beauty in a play which has, as images, much that is sombre and unpleasant. . . .

The Significance of Imagery

This method of working by way of suggestion, springing from a succession of vivid pictures and concrete details, is, of course, of the very essence of 'romantic' art; and, in the case of Shakespeare, the poet's mind, unlike the dyer's hand, subdues to itself what it works in, and colours with its dominating emotion all the varied material which comes his way, colours it so subtly and so delicately that for the most part we are unconscious of what is happening, and know only the total result of the effect on our imaginative sensibility.

Hence it seems to me that a study of his imagery from the angle from which we have just been looking at it, helps us to realise a little more fully and accurately one of the many ways by which he so magically stirs our emotions and excites our imagination, and I believe it not only does this, but that it sometimes even throws a fresh ray of light on the significance of the play concerned, and—most important of all—on the way Shakespeare himself saw it.

Claudius Turns the World Mad

Andrew Gurr

Andrew Gurr, a Shakespeare scholar, is professor of English at the University of Reading in England. In addition to his many books, including The Shakespearean Stage *and* Shakespearean Opposites, *he is director of Globe Research.*

To the Elizabethans, the head was regarded as the heavenly part of man, offering him the divine gifts of speech and reason. In Gurr's analysis in this selection, Hamlet's description of his head as a "distracted globe" becomes a metaphor for the entire play. Claudius's crimes do not just distract Hamlet's head from its normal functioning; they also turn all apparent values upside down. The play becomes a conflict between Hamlet's moral universe and Claudius's world of appearance, corruption, and villainy. With Hamlet finally inspired to action, the question arises: How does one get rid of a tyrant without becoming morally tainted? Or, to what extent does the end justify the means? In such a world, innocent people, like Ophelia, also become victims.

Hamlet's head, he tells us, is a "distracted globe". Alert like his creator to every nuance of situation and language, he captures in a single pun all three of the central features of the play. His metaphor is taken from the story of Hercules, the archetypal man of action, who took on his shoulders the burden of the heavens, the celestial globe carried by Atlas. The burden on Hamlet's shoulders is his own head, a globe more lunatic than heavenly, distracted from its proper function by the discovery that his uncle has murdered his father the king. To Elizabethans a man's head was the "heavenly" part of him, containing God's twin gifts of speech and reason, the qualities which raise man above the beasts. Fratricide and regicide, the murder of a king by his brother, were such ungodly acts as to "distract" any man's head from its proper functions of honest speech and moral reasoning.

Corruption Leads to Insanity

But when Hamlet speaks of "*this* distracted globe", and clutches his head with the pain of it, his thought is not only self-centred. The sphere he inhabits, the earthly globe, must be lunatic too if such things can happen in it. The world is not the moral and rational place that it should be. Claudius the murderer, and all the apparatus of the obedient court which surrounds and supports him, represent a world which has turned its proper values upside down. At the end of the play, when Hamlet ostensibly apologises to Laertes for the lunatic slaughter of his father Polonius, he obliquely accuses Claudius of madness. Crime is a form of insanity, since to destroy goodness and distract the world from its moral courses calls for an inversion of true reason. To invert moral values is ultimately insane, says Hamlet.

Hamlet's is a double metaphor, of distraction in the world at large and a distraction in his head mirroring the larger disorder. . . .

Conflict Between Inner and Outer Worlds

In essence the play exhibits the conflict between Hamlet's inner world, his acute sense of a moral universe governing human conduct, and the outside world of Claudius's government. Claudius's is the world of appearances, of polite seeming which can smile and smile and be villainous. Claudius is the man who puts his ambition before moral government, the proper use of the divine gift of reason. Hamlet is the man who sees through all the pretences, the "seeming" and "acting", so that his mind mirrors in anguish all the monstrous imperfections of the globe around him. Added to that anguish is the knowledge that because he alone sees the imperfections for what they are he alone can act to correct them. And by doing so he will inevitably be drawn into that imperfect globe. In an imperfect world the only means to correct imperfections are themselves imperfect. Hamlet has to do evil to correct evil. In that way his distraction is a true mirror of the madness of the Claudian world.

The context for *Hamlet* therefore, seen from a modern perspective, is the ageless debate over whether ends justify means. The absolute morality of a Hamlet, faced with the expedient ruthlessness of a Claudius, makes him choose between ruthless action of the kind Claudius excels in and suffering in private. His choice will depend on his decision whether the end of destroying Claudius can justify the means he must adopt if he is to succeed. He could suffer under this monstrous hypocrite or he could commit murder. No other course was really open to him.

In this small capsule Shakespeare fitted the whole political question that lay at the heart of sixteenth-century thinking about monarchies. When authority to govern is in the hands of one man, and he has that authority for the whole of his natural life, practical restraints on his use of that authority are difficult to maintain. The law gets its authority from him, so the law can't be used against him without losing that authority. More practically, since he controls law enforcement, who is to enforce it against him if he should choose to break it? ...

Moral Action in an Immoral World

To this theoretical and practical question, what circumstances might justify an individual taking the law into his own hands and committing regicide, Shakespeare applied *Hamlet*. He picked up the popular blood and thunder tradition of the revenge play and gave it a moral resonance by putting the emphasis not on the blood but on the individual's quandary between tyrannicide and the alternative virtue of Christian suffering, leaving vengeance to God. . . .

Hamlet is unique among Shakespeare's tragic heroes in being totally innocent himself of any crime when the play's action begins. He is called on to execute Claudius for his crime through no more complicity than being a blood relation of the victim of the crime. . . .

The Moral Hamlet

The moral component is there in Hamlet's thinking. He is continually aware of man's moral "capability and godlike reason" and in how beastlike a way the inhabitants of the Claudian world misuse it. But swamping that consciousness are the tides of his own blood and the passion of his response to Claudius's crime, a passion he can see no ready means of translating into moral action. Moral uncertainty is a mental process not easily separable from emotional incapacity. His moral consciousness is implicit in his reference to the "distracted", irrational globe; in his concern for man's honesty; in his eventual and reluctant acceptance of his role as "scourge and minister", God's instrument to punish the tyrant; and in many other oblique allusions to the moral aspect of his task as revenger. . . .

Conscience

One of the lesser marvels of *Hamlet* is how neatly the minutest details tally with the structure as a whole. Single words and phrases unerringly reflect the pattern of the drama in which they are set, as the single head of Hamlet reflects the world he inhabits. This confronts the modern reader with an obvious initial difficulty, since many of his key words have lost some of their meanings since his day. We may note, for instance, that Hamlet insists on using the word "conscience" where we might expect . . . that he would use "justice". That usage would seem less significant if we did not know the link between conscience as moral awareness and the "reason" (moral thought) which Hamlet regards as man's highest gift. Claudius has a bad conscience; Hamlet has a good one, but a conscience which means his ability to think morally, not just one free of guilt for wrongdoing, a "clear" conscience in our sense. The cowardice which he accuses himself of in all three of the soliloquies he delivers after learning the ghost's message is the outward appearance of an inward moral scruple, the "conscience" or thinking power which "doth make cowards of us *all*", because we all have that power if we care to use it. . . .

The Case of Ophelia

Ophelia's disaster stems from the doubt shared by her father and brother whether she would be an acceptable partner in marriage for Hamlet, since he is the heir apparent. Claudius proclaims Hamlet his heir in I.ii. In I.iii Laertes and Polonius both warn Ophelia to hold Hamlet off because he is a prince "out of thy star". She consequently returns Hamlet's gifts and gives him thereby a reason to display his lunatic disposition. Polonius jumps to the conclusion that Hamlet is mad because his love was rejected, and dies because he is still trying to spy on Hamlet to prove his theory when Hamlet has moved on from acting to action. Only when father and daughter are both dead does Gertrude casually prove the original doubt to have no foundation when she tells the corpse of Ophelia that she had hoped to see her married to Hamlet. . . .

The central characters form a double pattern. The love triangle of old Hamlet, Gertrude and adulterous Claudius turns into the hate triangle of Claudius, Gertrude and avenging Hamlet. Claudius as murder victim takes the place of old Hamlet, the original murder victim, and Hamlet takes Claudius's place as murderer. . . . Ophelia in her madness draws parallels too, with songs and flowers, when she muddles her dead father with a dead lover and sees her lover as forsaking her and as a wandering pilgrim. Laertes' revenge too becomes the image of Hamlet's own cause in Hamlet's eyes, another outbreak of the general infection.

Corruption Is a Progressive, Pervasive Disease

Derek Antona Traversi

Derek Antona Traversi's numerous articles and books on Shakespeare, *including* Shakespeare: The Roman Plays *and* Shakespeare: The Last Phase *had a strong influence on scholars in the 1960s and 1970s. Traversi died in 2005 in England.*

In the following selection, Traversi shows William Shakespeare imposing upon Hamlet *the plot of a revenge story, which usually involves rapid, bloody action. In this case, however, the revenge play is an inner exploration, which ironically delays action. The message of the ghost inspires both action and delay, in a complex play of politics, psychology, and ethics. These factors come to bear upon Hamlet's mind, as he is plunged, by the very nature of his self-exploration and the circumstances, into confusion and doubt. This sense of unease and foreboding—present from the very first scene, with the soldier on watch—never abates. On the political level, Claudius generates corruption with murder, espionage, and cruelty in his pursuit of power, poisoning all the characters. In a malfunctioning, dislocated state, Hamlet, in his drive for revenge, uses the same cruelties.*

In pursuing the duty laid upon him by his father's ghost, Hamlet brings to light a state of disease which affects the entire field presented to his consciousness; and, in the various stages through which this infection, this "imposthume," is exposed, he explores progressively the depths of his own infirmity.

In accordance with this conception, the first part of the play gradually concentrates its latent discords upon the revela-

Derek Antona Traversi, *An Approach to Shakespeare.* New York: Doubleday & Company, Inc., 1969. Copyright © 1956 by Doubleday & Company, Inc. Copyright © 1960, 1969 by Derek A. Traversi. All rights reserved. Used by permission of the publisher.

tion of the Ghost. This is not, as we may assume it to have been in the original melodrama, a simple call to action, an unambiguous appeal to filial piety; nor, on the other hand, can Hamlet's attitude toward it be accounted for, as some writers have argued, principally by his uncertainty as to the nature, good or evil, "heavenly" or "hellish" in its origins, of its inspiration. The matter is more complex than either of these attitudes would suggest, more closely related to the intimate contradictions of the play. *Both* aspects are in some degree relevant to a proper understanding of the Ghost, and the link that unites them is to be sought ultimately in Hamlet's own mind. The Ghost, in fact, acts upon Hamlet as a disturbing influence, imposing upon him a clear-cut filial obligation, to which all that is positive in his being responds, at the same time that it confirms the presence around him of sinister realities which he feels, even as he repudiates them, to be obscurely related to stresses in his own nature. In this way, far from leading to resolution through the action proposed by the original story, its message plunges the hero and his surroundings into obscurity and doubt.

Obscurity and doubt, indeed, accompany the first appearances of the Ghost. Horatio says that at the cockcrow "it started like a *guilty* thing", and that its coming "bodes some strange eruption" to the state. This "eruption" is present as an ill-defined foreboding in the minds of those who await its coming on the battlements of Elsinore. Francisco, the common soldier, is "sick at heart", and his "sickness," after finding an external projection in the feverish preparations for war reported by Marcellus, is more intimately related to the latent tensions of the play in Horatio's account of the threat from Norway which has inspired them:

young Fortinbras,

Of unimproved metal *hot* and *full*,

Hath in the skirts of Norway, here and there,

> *Shark't up* a list of *lawless* resolutes,
>
> For *food* and *diet*, to some enterprise
>
> That hath a stomach in't.

This type of imagery, describing social maladies in terms of the unbalance which "blood"-inspired "appetite" provokes in normal physical processes, links *Hamlet* in spirit to the other problem plays. Its dramatic counterpart is the revolt, repeatedly revealed in the course of the action, of youth against age, impulse against experience, restless self-will against the complacency of established authority. Fortinbras is expressly described as a young man defying his "impotent and bed-rid" uncle in pursuit of his own predatory ends. His behavior, which provokes from Denmark the correspondingly tense and strained reaction implied in Marcellus' talk of "sweaty haste" and "nightly" toil, will be paralleled by that of Laertes and, in a certain sense (in so far as Claudius claims "parental" tutelage over his nephew), of Hamlet himself; they point to a widespread dislocation of natural functioning, centered ultimately upon the inversion of normal relationships which accompanies the usurped royalty of the Danish king.

Abscess at the Heart of the Court

At this point it is well to bear firmly in mind, as we follow the deliberately slow and intricate development of the action, with its sense of plot and counterplot, its references to the "old mole" working below the surface of the earth and to the "enginer" "hoist with his own petard", that *Hamlet* is something more than the inwardly directed tragedy of an exceptionally complex and self-aware individual. Not all criticism of the play has recognized sufficiently the importance of its *political* aspect, the fact that its hero is, whatever else he may also be, a public figure, a prince and an heir apparent, whose relation to Claudius is colored from the outset by the ambiguous relationship in which they stand with respect to one another.

In this 1994 theater production of Hamlet *at the Open Air Theatre in England, Hamlet (Damian Lewis) holds a sword over the kneeling Claudius (Paul Freeman). Hamlet's revenge on his uncle is not bloody and swift, but rather a conclusion to an inner exploration in which Hamlet contemplates the meaning of life and death.* © Robbie Jack/Corbis.

When Hamlet, on his initial appearance, stands pointedly aside in the presence of his uncle's assembled court, listening to the flow of bland, respectable commonplace which comes so readily and, it seems, so impressively from the throne, and inserts from time to time the obscure comments which reflect what is to us his still unexplained bitterness—"I am too much i' the sun"; "A little more than kin and less than kind"—it is not the barbaric drama of some remote Danish principality that stirs our interest but something nearer both to Shakespeare and ourselves: the intrigue and the treachery that accompanied the maneuvering for power in a Renaissance court. Beneath Claudius' impressive ability to assume, on the surface and in the public eye, the appropriately judicious and authoritative mask, which has even led some students of the play to minimize the full extent of his malignity, lie the obsessive realities of insecurity, ruthlessness, and hunger for power which it is Hamlet's tragedy that he can only meet on their own level, by answering spying with counterespionage, cruelty with the deliberate suppression of pity, and usurpation with murder. By so doing, by experiencing to the full the claustrophobic quality of this corrupt and unnatural court, he finally exposes the "imposthume" [abscess] implicit in Claudius' rule and rids Denmark of the poison at its heart; but this is not accomplished before he has himself been destroyed by his recognition of the link which binds him, in his own despite, to the reality he is called upon to destroy. . . .

Dislocation of Family

Polonius' treatment of his children, and their contrasted reactions to him, rebellious and unnaturally submissive respectively, indicate in the personal order the profound dislocation of normal relationships which prevails beneath the bland surface of Claudius' rule and extends like a stain over the entire field of his authority. . . .

Corruption of Love

His father's love for his mother had, as their son now recalls it, a precarious artificial quality, as though its object needed to be protected from physical contact, even to the extent of not permitting the wind to "visit" her face "too roughly"; but her response to it is associated, still in his memory, with a passionate intensity of craving . . . :

> she would hang on him,
>
> As if *increase of appetite* had grown
>
> By what it *fed* on. (I. ii)

Such a passage will show why some critics have found the emotion expressed in *Hamlet* excessive, imperfectly related to its causes as dramatically presented. It is—be it noted—Gertrude's relation to her first, not her "incestuous," husband that is being recalled; and the impression conveyed is not that of a particular, unlawful relationship, nor even simply of the sensual weakness which has borne fruit in his mother's infatuation for Claudius, but of a corruption present at the heart of passion and affecting all human relationships. That corruption, both in love and in the experience which finds in love one particularly intense expression, seeks in this tragedy an adequate dramatic projection. . . .

The Pervasiveness of Claudius's Contamination

The contamination produced by association with Claudius' rule affects to some degree all those who surround him, so that none—from the moment of his self-betrayal—can live at ease with himself or his surroundings. All of them, indeed, are involved through Hamlet's bitter asides in the falsity, the inner hollowness, of the central situation. The appearance of ordered peace hitherto offered by his uncle's rule having been finally destroyed, his nephew is ready to probe ever deeper into the corruption which surrounds him and which, as we have seen, ultimately covers the central action as a reflection of his own state. . . .

The last scene reflects the spirit which, in greater or less degree, has prevailed throughout the play. Hamlet's efforts to follow the course of duty have been throughout obstructed by an inner conflict, a settled disgust, the true extent of which is only gradually revealed in the course of the action. This conflict, or disgust, is spread through the entire tragedy, into which it instills a pervasive, violent poison, associated in some degree with the disorder of the "blood" in and through which it works. The poison is present in all the protagonists and in the state which is their common environment; but it works always *from within* outward, revealing its full power to destroy in the course of its development. It is supremely present beneath the suave surface of Claudius, whose usurped authority is undermined in the course of the play by guilt and fear; but it is also present in Gertrude, whose weakness has led to the marriage which her son, finding in it an exterior projection of his inner disgust, regards as "incestuous." It can be found in the senile self-regard of Polonius, more especially in his attitude toward youth and passion, and eventually breaks through to the surface in the madness of the shattered Ophelia; Laertes, the representative of hot, idle youth, shares it, and so does even the active, confident Fortinbras in his irresponsible military adventures. Above all, it is present in Hamlet himself, whose actions throughout are peculiarly calculated to bring about its exposure in those around him. By the end of the play Hamlet has revealed all the evils which surround him and has shown them to be variously, if obscurely, related to the stresses, which constitute the real center of the tragedy, in his own soul. By bringing them to the light, and by finally carrying out as a passive instrument the mission imposed upon him, he leads those who surround him, with himself, to the death that is their common end. The spirit of this tragedy is still involved in contradiction, still imperfect in its clarity of conception; but never so far in Shakespeare's work has an emotional situation been so variously reflected in an elaborate dramatic action. The fact is of decisive importance for an understanding of the dramatist's complete development.

Hamlet Is Corrupt, Not Claudius

G. Wilson Knight

G. Wilson Knight (1897–1985) was a scholar as well as a producer of and actor in Shakespearean plays. He taught at the University of Leeds in England for more than twenty years. Among his many books are Shakespeare Production *and* Myth and Miracle.

In the following essay Knight concentrates on Hamlet's spiritual and mental condition. While recognizing the causes of Hamlet's turmoil—his father's murder, his mother's presumed incest, and Claudius's assumption of a crown that belonged to him—Knight sees the play and its values in terms of practicality. Thus Hamlet is a mentally disturbed troublemaker obsessed with death and cynicism and a rejecter of love and life, as his scenes with Ophelia illustrate. Claudius, then, emerges as a "good king" who has repented of his past crime and now rules with efficient common sense, in actions that represent a love of life and commitment to the well-being of Denmark. According to Knight, the enemy of Denmark is Hamlet, who would have benefited everyone and himself by just leaving things alone.

To Hamlet the light has been extinguished from things of earth. He has lost all sense of purpose. We already know one reason for Hamlet's state: his father's death. Claudius and his mother have already urged him to

> throw to earth
>
> This unprevailing woe . . .

G. Wilson Knight, *The Wheel of Fire: Interpretations of Shakespearean Tragedy with Three New Essays*. Andover, Hampshire: Methuen & Co. Ltd., 1959. Reproduced by permission of the publisher.

Now, during Hamlet's soliloquy, we see another reason: disgust at his mother's second marriage:

> ... within a month:
>
> Ere yet the salt of most unrighteous tears
>
> Had left the flushing in her galled eyes,
>
> She married. O, most wicked speed, to post
>
> With such dexterity to incestuous sheets!

Learning of the Unweeded Garden

These two concrete embodiments of Hamlet's misery are closely related. He suffers from misery at his father's death and agony at his mother's quick forgetfulness: such callousness is infidelity, and so impurity, and, since Claudius is the brother of the King, incest. It is reasonable to suppose that Hamlet's state of mind, if not wholly caused by these events, is at least definitely related to them. Of his two loved parents, one has been taken for ever by death, the other dishonoured for ever by her act of marriage. To Hamlet the world is now an 'unweeded garden'. ...

Nor is this all. He next learns that his father's murderer now wears the crown, is married to his faithless mother. Both elements in his original pain are thus horribly intensified. His hope of recovery to the normal state of healthy mental life depended largely on his ability to forget his father, to forgive his mother. Claudius advised him well. Now his mother's honour is more foully smirched than ever; and the living cause and symbol of his father's death is firmly placed on Denmark's throne. ...

Loss of Meaning and Hope

Hamlet, when we first meet him, has lost all sense of life's significance. To a man bereft of the sense of purpose there is no possibility of creative action, it has no meaning. No act but suicide is rational. Yet to Hamlet comes the command of a great act—revenge: therein lies the unique quality of the play—a sick soul is commanded to heal, to cleanse, to create harmony. But good cannot come of evil: it is seen that the sickness of his soul only further infects the state—his disintegration spreads out, disintegrating.

Hamlet's soul is sick to death—and yet there was one thing left that might have saved him. In the deserts of his mind, void with the utter vacuity of the knowledge of death—death of his father, death of his mother's faith—was yet one flower, his love of Ophelia. . . .

The love of Ophelia is thus Hamlet's last hope. This, too, is taken from him. Her repelling of his letters and refusing to see him, in obedience to Polonius' command, synchronizes unmercifully with the terrible burden of knowledge laid on Hamlet by the revelation of the Ghost. . . .

Poisoning of Love

Hamlet denies the existence of romantic values. Love, in his mind, has become synonymous with sex, and sex with uncleanness. Therefore beauty is dangerous and unclean. Sick of the world, of man, of love, Hamlet denies the reality of his past romance: 'I loved you not'. This statement alone fits coherently into his diseased mind, and so it is, to him, the truth. He cannot have loved, since love is unreal: if it were real, there would be meaning, passion, purpose in existence. These things are gone and love must go too. . . .

The Shadow of Death

The horror of humanity doomed to death and decay has disintegrated Hamlet's mind. From the first scene to the last the shadow of death broods over this play. In the exquisite prose threnody [poem or song of mourning] of the Graveyard scene the thought of physical death is again given utterance. There its pathos, its inevitability, its moral, are emphasized: but also its hideousness. Death is indeed the theme of this play, for Hamlet's disease is mental and spiritual death. So Hamlet, in his most famous soliloquy, concentrates on the terrors of an after life. The uninspired, devitalized intellect of a Hamlet thinks pre-eminently in terms of time. To him, the body disintegrates in time; the soul persists in time too; and both are horrible. His consciousness, functioning in terms of evil and negation, sees Hell but not Heaven. But the intuitive faith, or love, or purpose, by which we must live if we are to remain sane, of these things, which are drawn from a timeless reality within the soul, Hamlet is unmercifully bereft. Therefore he dwells on the foul appearances of sex, the hideous decay of flesh, the deceit of beauty either of the spirit or of the body, the torments of eternity if eternity exist. The universe is an 'unweeded garden', or a 'prison', the canopy of the sky but a 'pestilent congregation of vapours', and man but a 'quintessence of dust', waiting for the worms of death.

It might be objected that I have concentrated unduly on the unpleasant parts of the play. It has been my intention to concentrate. They are the most significant parts. I have tried by various quotations and by suggestive phrases to indicate this sickness which eats into Hamlet's soul. . . . Now by emphasizing these elements in the figure of Hamlet I have essayed to pluck out the heart of his mystery. And it will be clear that the elements which I have emphasized, the matter of Hamlet's madness, his patent cruelty, his coarse humour, his strange dialogue with Ophelia, his inability to avenge his father's death, are all equally related to the same sickness within. . . .

Claudius Is Human, Hamlet Inhuman

Throughout the first half of the play Claudius is the typical kindly uncle, besides being a good king. His advice to Hamlet about his exaggerated mourning for his father's death is admirable common sense:

Fie! 'Tis a fault to Heaven,

A fault against the dead, a fault to nature,

To reason most absurd; whose common theme

Is death of fathers, and who still hath cried,

From the first corse, till he that died to-day,

'This must be so.'

It is the advice of worldly common sense opposed to the extreme misery of a sensitive nature paralysed by the facts of death and unfaithfulness. This contrast points the relative significance of the King and his court to Hamlet. They are of the world—with their crimes, their follies, their shallownesses, their pomp and glitter; they are of humanity, with all its failings, it is true, but yet of humanity. They assert the importance of human life, they believe in it, in themselves. Whereas Hamlet is inhuman, since he has seen through the tinsel of life and love, he believes in nothing, not even himself, except the memory of a ghost, and his black-robed presence is a reminder to everyone of the fact of death. There is no question but that Hamlet is right. The King's smiles hide murder, his mother's love for her new consort is unfaithfulness to Hamlet's father, Ophelia has deserted Hamlet at the hour of his need. Hamlet's philosophy may be inevitable, blameless, and irrefutable. But it is the negation of life. It is death. Hence Hamlet is a continual fear to Claudius, a reminder of his crime. It is a mistake to consider Claudius as a hardened criminal. . . .

Claudius, as he appears in the play, is not a criminal. He is—strange as it may seem—a good and gentle king, enmeshed by the chain of causality linking him with his crime. And this chain he might, perhaps, have broken except for Hamlet, and all would have been well. But, granted the presence of Hamlet—which Claudius at first genuinely desired, persuading him not to return to Wittenberg as he wished—and granted the fact of his original crime which cannot now be altered, Claudius can hardly be blamed for his later actions. They are forced on him. As King, he could scarcely be expected to do otherwise. Hamlet is a danger to the state, even apart from his knowledge of Claudius' guilt. He is an inhuman—or superhuman—presence, whose consciousness— . . . is centred on death. . . .

Morality of Claudius and Hamlet

The question of the relative morality of Hamlet and Claudius reflects the ultimate problem of this play. . . .

[Claudius's] problems are indeed overwhelming. When Laertes enters, Claudius rouses our admiration by his cool reception of him:

What is the cause, Laertes,

That thy rebellion looks so giant-like?

Let him go, Gertrude; do not fear our person:

There's such divinity doth hedge a king,

That treason can but peep to what it would,

Acts little of its will. Tell me, Laertes,

Why thou art thus incensed. Let him go, Gertrude.

Speak, man.

When he hears of Hamlet's return he plots treachery with Laertes. Everything considered, one can hardly blame him. . . . He has, it is true, committed a dastardly murder, but in the play he gives us the impression of genuine penitence and a host of good qualities. After the murder of Polonius we certainly feel that both the King and the Queen are sane and doing their level best to restrain the activities of a madman. That is the impression given by the play at this point, as we read. If we think in terms of logic, we remember at once that we must side with Hamlet; and we perhaps remember the continual and sudden emergences of a different Hamlet, a Hamlet loving and noble and sane. But intermittent madness is more dangerous by far than obvious insanity. At the best we only prove that Hamlet's madness is justifiable, a statement which makes nonsense; for Hamlet's behaviour, so utterly out of harmony with his environment of eminently likeable people, in that relation may well be called a kind of madness. Whatever it is, it is extremely dangerous and powerful.

I have concentrated on Claudius' virtues. They are manifest. So are his faults—his original crime, his skill in the less admirable kind of policy, treachery, and intrigue. But I would point clearly that, in the movement of the play, his faults are forced on him, and he is distinguished by creative and wise action, a sense of purpose, benevolence, a faith in himself and those around him, by love of his Queen. . . .

But Hamlet is not of flesh and blood, he is a spirit of penetrating intellect and cynicism and misery, without faith in himself or anyone else, murdering his love of Ophelia, on the brink of insanity, taking delight in cruelty, torturing Claudius, wringing his mother's heart, a poison in the midst of the healthy bustle of the court. He is a superman among men. And he is a superman because he has walked and held converse with death, and his consciousness works in terms of death and the negation of cynicism. He has seen the truth, not alone of Denmark, but of humanity, of the universe: and the truth is evil. Thus Hamlet is an element of evil in the state of Denmark. The poison of his mental existence spreads outwards among things of flesh and blood, like acid eating into metal. They are helpless before his very inactivity and fall one after the other, like victims of an infectious disease. They are strong with the strength of health—but the demon of Hamlet's mind is a stronger thing than they. Futilely they try to get him out of their country; anything to get rid of him, he is not safe. . . .

The Welfare of Denmark

If we think primarily of the state of Denmark during the action of the play, we are bound to applaud Claudius, as he appears before us: he acts throughout with a fine steadiness of purpose. By creating normal and healthy and lovable persons around his protagonist, whose chief peculiarity is the abnormality of extreme melancholia, the poet divides our sympathies. The villain has become a kindly uncle, the princely hero is the incarnation of cynicism. It is true that if Hamlet had promptly avenged his father, taken the throne, forgotten his troubles, resumed a healthy outlook on life, he would have all our acclamations. Laertes entering in wrath at the death of his father, during 'damnation' and threatening Claudius, comes on us like a blast of fresh air, after the stifling, poisonous atmosphere of Hamlet's mind. Laertes and Hamlet struggling at Ophelia's grave are like symbols of life and death contending for the prize of love. Laertes is brave in his course of loyalty. But to expect such a course from Hamlet is to misunderstand him quite and his place in the play. The time is out of joint, he is thrown out of any significant relation with his world. He cannot bridge the gulf by rational action. Nor can he understand the rest any more than they understand him. His ideals—which include an insistent memory of death—are worth nothing to them, and, most maddening fact of all, they get on perfectly well as they are—or would do if Hamlet were out of the way. Thus, through no fault of his own, Hamlet has been forced into a state of evil: Claudius, whose crime originally placed him there, is in a state of healthy and robust spiritual life. Hamlet, and we too, are perplexed.

The Corruption of Reason

Juliet McLauchlan

Juliet McLauchlan is the author of Shakespeare: Othello *and a study of Thomas Hardy. She was also the founder of the Joseph Conrad Society.*

In the following selection, McLauchlan contends that Claudius has corrupted the state of Denmark before Hamlet *begins, so when Hamlet comes onto the scene, he is in conflict between the idealism he has been taught at Wittenberg and the cold practicality of Denmark, where Claudius has become the state, in true Elizabethan fashion. McLauchlan argues that at first Hamlet aspires to and represents the Renaissance man, in whom reason rules passion. But Hamlet's loss of balance leaves him less than a complete man, and he becomes more swayed by passion than reason. Finally, McLauchlan concludes, it is apparent that the whole situation—the evil both around and within Hamlet—is hopeless, and nothing, not even reason, will bring order and light to the state and its citizens.*

When *Hamlet* begins, someone other than the hero has already violated the natural order of the kingdom, and the hero, although profoundly disturbed, is only partially aware of the evil which is entrenched. Hamlet's original 'intent' to go back to Wittenberg seems to reflect a feeling of helplessness and a desire simply to escape from Elsinore as it now is. Agreeing to stay, he rightly senses that 'it is not, nor it cannot come to good'. Thus, for the hero of *Hamlet*, the situation is from the very start one of tragic disruption: to see the play in terms of a conflict which shatters the prince when he is faced

Juliet McLauchlan, *Aspects of Hamlet: Articles Reprinted from Shakespeare Survey*. New York: Cambridge University Press, 1979. This collection copyright © Cambridge University Press 1979. Reprinted with the permission of Cambridge University Press and the author.

with life in the Denmark of Claudius constitutes a key approach—not a new one, but, as I hope to demonstrate, one which it is illuminating to carry further. In this play Shakespeare creates and intensifies the sense of tragic conflict by particularly subtle and oblique *presentation* of concepts of the universe, the state, and man, which were familiar in his day. . . .

My argument will seek to show that Shakespeare presents in *Hamlet* a conflict between the humanistic Wittenberg ideal with its upward aspirations, and the negation of it at Elsinore. He shows this ideal to have been Hamlet's and to have been embodied for him in the figure of his father, 'a man, take him for all in all, / I shall not look upon his like again'. . . .

Wittenberg's Idealism vs. Elsinore's Corruption

Hamlet has seen life in the idealistic light of this concept of following the 'way up'. To this exalted ideal he suffers a shattering blow, which proves tragic in its effects upon him: we see the disintegration of his own wholeness as a man and, worse, watch his responses to the evil around him, responses which are passionate and ultimately destructive to others and to himself, rather than rational. It is what Hamlet suffers, is, and does in the course of the play, which pre-eminently constitutes the tragedy of *Hamlet*.

The second concept basic to my argument is that the king served (under God) as head of the body politic, and the health of this body depended upon the virtue of the king. . . .

These long-held and much-discussed concepts involved the conviction that a violation of any one part of the natural order of things must bring disruption into the rest. . . .

In *Hamlet* we see, mainly through the two protagonists, the shattering of familiar Renaissance (and earlier) ideals through conflict with . . . a world where the weapon of man's reason is not adequately used (by Hamlet) and where, in any case, it seems that reason would be powerless to 'set it right'.

Emphasising the conflict, deep ironies arise from the fact that the traditional positives of kingship and of man's potential are often expressed at Elsinore by those whose behaviour and values are a negation of what is asserted. Furthermore, there is sometimes more than the usual degree of irony when a character speaks more truly than he realises. Claudius, for instance, refers to Fortinbras as:

> Holding a weak supposal of our worth,
>
> Or thinking by our late dear brother's death
>
> Our state to be disjoint and out of frame

His sarcastic words imply his own worth and the health of his state; yet a weak supposal of Claudius would be the right one, and his Denmark *is* 'disjoint' and 'out of frame' precisely by his brother's death—or rather by the manner of it. While the court is completely taken in, Shakespeare would not intend his audience to miss the irony. . . .

Corruption of the Natural Order

By Claudius's violation of the natural order, his state is 'rotten' and evil is established. He has murdered the rightful king, who was also his brother; although his marriage to the dead king's widow has been sanctioned by the court, Elizabethans would see it as incest, and this in itself would cast doubt upon the king's smooth explanations; similarly, although his accession has been formally approved according to Danish custom, the Ghost soon reveals that he is, in the spirit if not the letter, a usurper. . . .

The most extraordinary thing about Claudius is the blandness with which he assumes that he has become, in the true sense, 'Denmark'. He speaks as if he sees himself firmly within the order which his deeds have grossly violated. Gertrude, too, entirely accepts this; true, she is not aware of his crime, but it is a serious indictment of a weak and obtuse nature that she can beg her grieving son to 'look like a friend on Denmark'. . . .

"Consummate Toadies"

When Rosencrantz and Guildenstern arrive they vie with each other in piling phrase upon obsequious phrase. Rosencrantz declares that the 'majesties' of Denmark could by their 'sovereign power' put their 'dread pleasures' into commands instead of simply requesting service. Guildenstern rushes to add: 'But we both obey', finishing off Rosencrantz's line, and the rest of his words follow headlong:

> And here give up ourselves, in the full bent,
>
> To lay our service freely at your feet,
>
> To be commanded.

It is part of the subtlety of Shakespeare's presentation of Claudius's court and state that these two consummate toadies should try to express the true positives of kingship, and particularly (again) the mystical unity between king and body politic. . . .

Claudius's appearance of kingship is shown here in all its worthlessness. Hamlet is, of course, putting into precise perspective the extravagant words of Rosencrantz and Guildenstern, but what is more interesting is that the audience has no need of a nudge from Hamlet in order to judge them. What it does need is to see Hamlet's awareness of the nature of their relationship to the king and to see that this is part of his justified loathing of all that Elsinore has come to stand for since his father's death. . . .

Hamlet's Degeneration

While he cannot and should not acquiesce in such a denial of the natural order as would make him truly heir to a murderous usurping 'uncle-father', he must remain virtually imprisoned in this false court situation so long as he fails to come to terms with the duty laid upon him by his father's spirit. Conflicts within himself delay this so that the state is not finally purged until after Ophelia is dead (largely by Hamlet's fault, although she is not herself blameless)—too late, that is, for any restoration of the 'fair state' with Hamlet at its head, for the link between Ophelia and Hamlet (as the state's 'expectancy') is crucial to the future. . . .

Hamlet sees the underlying court situation as evil because his ideal of kingship is inseparable from his ideal of 'a man'. The sort of a king a man will make depends upon the sort of man he is. Hamlet mourns his father as 'so excellent a king', with all the force of the word 'excellent', but it is his father as a man and as his mother's husband that he most reveres in memory. . . .

How far is this ideal really established in relation to old Hamlet? . . . Two-points seem relevant: the 'rotten' state must somehow be purged of its evil; the demand of the soldier-king is made in terms of an accepted code, such as is followed without question by Laertes, and which is not questioned even by Hamlet himself. Old Hamlet takes on some of the attributes of the ideal king (and man) simply through deliberate contrasts with Claudius. . . .

The Ghost's last words seem to confirm the value of this husband's love, and the validity of Hamlet's view of it. He forgets his desire to spur his son to revenge and pleads with Hamlet to show compassion to his mother, his last words, 'Speak to her, Hamlet'.

The significance of this is that Hamlet's ideal of his father, and thus of man, seems to have been based upon his ideal view of his parents' marriage; his deep disillusionment with man and with life springs *primarily* from the shock to this ideal. Hamlet rightly sees an ugly degeneration from love to lust in Gertrude's second marriage, and it is certainly this, rather than the political disruption of Denmark, which disturbs Hamlet most and rouses his most passionate outbursts. . . .

Part of the tragedy of *Hamlet* lies then in our suffering with the prince in his deepening awareness of evil and in his consequent agonising loss of belief in man's potentialities. This is not the whole of it. In Elsinore, Hamlet's own personality, his embodiment of his own ideal, suffers disintegration. Ophelia's words of mournful remembrance are as crucial to the play as is Hamlet's great speech on the Renaissance ideal:

> Oh, what a noble mind is here o'erthrown!
>
> The courtier's, scholar's, soldier's, eye, tongue,
>
> sword,
>
> The expectancy and rose of the fair state,
>
> The glass of fashion, and the mould of form,
>
> The observed of all observers, quite, quite down!
>
> And I, of ladies most deject and wretched,
>
> That suck'd the honey of his music-vows,
>
> Now see that noble and most sovereign reason,
>
> Like sweet bells jangled out of tune, and harsh;
>
> That unmatch'd form and feature of blown youth
>
> Blasted with ecstasy

The more we imagine the whole man, as she recalls him, the more we feel the tragedy. Courtier, soldier, scholar—of this Renaissance prince there are only glimpses. . . .

Corruption Encompasses All

The tragedy of *Hamlet* goes further than the disintegration of the Renaissance prince. The evil, the 'imposthume' in the Danish royal family and state, so horrifies Hamlet that it evokes evil in response. The corruption of personality, family, and state is as ugly as Hamlet thinks it is, but the upsurge of evil within him is ugly too and destructive. Hamlet, whose ideal is 'that man that is not passion's slave', who believes that reason and moderation (like Horatio's) should control passion, becomes almost obsessed by hatred of evil, and is more often swayed by passion than ruled by reason. How can we account for this?

In his last soliloquy, he passionately and half-despairingly asserts, in very characteristic terms, the value of reason:

> What is a man,
>
> If the chief good and market of his time
>
> Be but to sleep and feed? a beast, no more;
>
> Sure, he that made us with such large discourse,
>
> Looking before and after, gave us not
>
> That capability and god-like reason
>
> To fust in us unus'd.

Surely, he asks, man should not be just a beast? Surely he must use his reason? And Hamlet has been using his reason. Or has he? Later in this soliloquy he wonders if he may have been thinking 'too precisely upon the event'; if so, there is little evidence of it when we see Hamlet in thought or action, nor have we often seen him reasoning out alternative courses of action. The first soliloquy is no reasoned assessment of the situation but a passionate outpouring of deep grief and bitter disgust, culminating in resigned acceptance of heartbreak and silent inactivity. To the encounter with the Ghost he responds more passionately than rationally. The second soliloquy includes a passionate response to the player's speech, a passionate denunciation of himself, a passionate outburst against Claudius, then more self-denunciation before he finally does set his brain to work on the idea of the play. 'To be or not to be' leads into a prolonged and complex meditation, rather than to concrete reasoning on specific problems. In the short soliloquy (III, 2) there is little reasoning, for Hamlet characteristically finds here some outlet in words, but is clearly swept by a passionate desire to act violently against his mother. Fear that he may actually do so leads him to resolve to exercise control. . . .

Do we then see in *Hamlet* a twofold failure of reason: (1) to show the prince how to deal with evident external evil and (2) to enable him to control evil within himself? I would argue, rather, that his passionate response to evil is so intense that for the most part reason is simply not invoked at all. Instead of reasoning, Hamlet habitually verbalises the emotions which spring from his deeply-felt failure to come to terms with the problem—*with a problem which in fact reason cannot solve*. Can reason show Hamlet any action which will restore an order which has been brutally and permanently destroyed? Old Hamlet is dead, Gertrude is 'one flesh' with the satyr who murdered him. Can the irreversible be reversed by any rational action? Even if reason should sanction the revenge to which passion prompts Hamlet (and this is never reasoned out) will this put things right?. . .

Too Much Destroyed

Despite Hamlet's few positive affirmations, we do not come to the end of the play with any conviction that the prince has attained higher understanding, or even regained wholeness as a human being. In the storm of evil, external and internal, in which he has been caught up, too much has been destroyed. This is not to say that 'the readiness is all' implies merely a fatalistic resignation or exhaustion, but Hamlet does seem in a sense spent. There is simplicity and beauty (but of a very ambiguous kind) in his last words, 'The rest is silence', no real affirmation. It is left to Horatio to confirm our feelings: despite all the degradation, the 'falling off' which we have watched in Hamlet in the course of the play, it is a 'noble heart' which has cracked; a 'sweet prince' has died. These comments do not sentimentalise Hamlet, but like Horatio's last prayer that 'flights of angels sing thee to thy rest', serve directly to link Hamlet once more with the great potential envisaged for Renaissance man. Indeed the whole man is once more evoked as both soldier and scholar praise in their own ways the dead prince. This constitutes a final and infinitely sad irony: in *Hamlet* the waste which is characteristic of tragedy is seen as a failure to fulfil a noble and precisely defined potential.

Corruption's Effect on Love

H.D.F. Kitto

H.D.F. Kitto (1897–1982) was professor of Greek at the University of Bristol in England. He is the author of five books on Greek drama.

In this essay, Kitto maintains that the evil of King Claudius and his court supporter, Polonius, not only leaves the country in disarray but also poisons love—what Kitto sees as the essence of goodness. Claudius and Gertrude have made a mockery of love in their incestuous marriage of convenience so soon after the death of Hamlet's father; the friendship between Hamlet and his friends, such as Rosencrantz, Guildenstern, and especially Laertes, has been tarnished irrevocably; Hamlet's love for his mother has been compromised; and, most telling of all, the love between Ophelia and Hamlet has been poisoned. What should have been lasting love ends in suffering and death. The ultimate, horrific scene illustrating and representing this pattern is the fight between Laertes and Hamlet in the open grave of Ophelia, Kitto asserts.

In *Hamlet*, eight people are killed, not counting Hamlet's father; of the two families concerned in the play, those of King Hamlet and Polonius, both are wiped out. Eight deaths are enough to attract attention, and to make us wonder if the essential thing has been said when the play is called 'the tragedy of a man who could not make up his mind'. And the manner of these deaths is no less significant than their number. Claudius murders King Hamlet by poison; thereafter, a metaphorical poison seeps through the play: rottenness, cankers, 'things rank and gross in nature' meet us at every turn. Then at the end it once more becomes literal poison: Ger-

H.D.F. Kitto, *Form and Meaning in Drama*. New York: Barnes and Noble, 1956.

trude, Claudius, Laertes, Hamlet are all poisoned; and on Claudius, already dead or dying from the poisoned rapier, Hamlet forces the poisoned cup. The Ghost had said:

> *Nor let thy soul contrive*

> *Against thy mother aught; leave her to Heaven.*

So too Horatio observed:

> *Heaven will direct it.*

And what does Heaven do with Gertrude? Of her own accord, and in spite of a warning, she drinks poison. These are plain and striking dramatic facts; how far does 'Hamlet's fatal indecision' explain them? Are they an organic part of a tragedy of character? Or did Shakespeare kill so many people merely from force of habit? . . .

Love Is Equivalent to Goodness

Hamlet is—or was—in love with Ophelia and she with him. . . . It will do us no harm to remember what Love so often is in Shakespeare: not merely a romantic emotion, but a symbol of goodness, even a redemptive power. We have been told often enough in the play what Claudius and Gertrude have made of Love; we ought to have noticed how Polonius thinks of it. In this scene the pure love of Ophelia is being used by two evil men who besmirch everything they touch. This would need argument—and plenty is available—except that in this very scene Shakespeare makes further argument unnecessary: Polonius gives Ophelia a book, evidently a holy book. Lying, spying, double-dealing, are second nature to this wise old counsellor; even so, the formal indecency of what he is doing now makes him uneasy. . . .

So, Polonius, there you are—and there too is Claudius, who also confesses at this moment the rottenness of his soul.

These two, then, for their own purposes exploit a young love and the exercise of devotion, sugaring o'er the Devil himself. At the end of the scene Polonius proposes to do the same thing again. He hides behind a second arras, and finds that to be too busy is some danger.

Evidently, the character of Hamlet and the death of Polonius are not unconnected, but it is not the case that Shakespeare contrived the latter merely to illustrate the former. The perspective is wider than this. If we will not see the 'divine background', whatever that may prove to be in this play, what shall we make of what Hamlet now says?—

> *For this same lord*
>
> *I do repent: but Heaven hath pleased it so,*
>
> *To punish me with this, and this with me,*
>
> *That I must be their scourge and minister.*

A shuffling-off of responsibility? No; this has the authentic ring of Greek, that is to say, of 'religious', tragedy. The deed is Hamlet's, and Hamlet must answer for it. But at the same time it is the work of Heaven; it is, so to speak, what *would* happen, what ought to happen, to a man who has been sugaring o'er the Devil himself. . . .

[The] sudden revelation of unsuspected depths of evil and treachery, together with the awful insecurity that it brings, are the very essence of Hamlet's tragedy. Whether he can 'make up his mind' or not, his mental and spiritual life lies in ruins.

> *There are more things in Heaven and Earth, Horatio,*
>
> *Than are dreamt of in your philosophy. . . .*

Infectious Evil Kills Love

Shakespeare makes Denmark a concentration of evil: 'Something is rotten in the state of Denmark'; 'At least, I'm sure it may be so in Denmark'; 'Is it a custom?—Ay, marry is't; but to my mind, though I am native here. . .' Later, when we hear

'Denmark's a prison' we hear these undertones too; it is a prison, full of evil—and Hamlet was denied leave to escape. He is locked up with evil; and more than that: it is for him alone to know, and to grapple with, the worst evil of all. . . .

Hamlet and Ophelia

Ophelia's tragedy is much more closely intertwined with Hamlet's than her brother's is. To understand it, we shall have to consider what Hamlet was, and what he has become; what a fair prospect there was, and why it ends in madness and death. We shall be led to the same conclusion: The King, the King's to blame; except that in this case two companions in evil, Gertrude and Polonius, contribute much. It is the 'unweeded garden' that does not allow Ophelia to flower. We will attempt to follow, though with necessary digressions, this joint tragedy.

> *Doubt thou the stars are fire;*
>
> *Doubt that the Sun doth move;*
>
> *Doubt truth to be a liar;*
>
> *But never doubt I love.*
>
> *O dear Ophelia, I am ill at these numbers; I have not art to reckon my groans; but that I love thee best, O most best, believe it.*

We know something of the unclouded Hamlet who wrote this love-letter, Hamlet as he was. Not only have we Ophelia's own heart-broken speech:

> *O what a noble mind is here o'erthrown. . .*

We also are given, from time to time, glimpses of the real Hamlet—at moments when, so to speak, he forgets; as, for example, when he so gaily welcomes, and jests with, Rosencrantz and Guildenstern, or the Players; or when he talks with such clean, good sense about the theatre. In his portrait of the essential Hamlet, Shakespeare has succeeded, as no one else, in putting before us a man of genius: the courtier, scholar, soldier; 'eye, tongue, sword'; the artist, the philosopher; the gay companion and the resolute man of action. . . .

Drama, as we have said before, is the art of significant juxtaposition. Over against these glimpses of Hamlet as he is by nature, Shakespeare sets his picture of Hamlet as he has now become, Hamlet 'mad'. Over against this promise of a happy love—

I hoped thou shoulds't have been my Hamlet's wife—

he sets the twisted, hideous thing that it has become. What twisted it, and what the connexion is between this and the rest of the play, is not hard to see. . . .

Ophelia's tragedy is that she is innocently obedient to a disastrous father; Hamlet's, in respect of Ophelia, is that Love has become confused with foulness, and that he knows not what he can trust.

He falls to such perusal of my face

As he would draw it.

Hamlet is taking farewell, not of Ophelia, but of love and innocence and goodness.

He seemed to find his way without his eyes,

For out o' doors he went without their help. 'Out o' doors'—into what? Into what Shakespeare is going to show us, time after time: into deliberate and bitter obscenity. . . . The rottenness in Denmark has corrupted Love itself. Upon which, Shakespeare turns on Polonius with savage irony. He makes the crass man say: 'This is the very ecstasy of love.' No it isn't; it is indeed ecstasy, as the word is used in this play, but it is the death of love. . . .

Hamlet (Mel Gibson) and Ophelia (Helena Bonham Carter) hold hands in this 1990 movie version of Hamlet. *The rampant corruption in* Hamlet *eventually poisons the love between Hamlet and Ophelia.* Paramount/The Kobal Collection/The Picture Desk, Inc.

The Perversion of Love

Love happens to be one of Shakespeare's symbols of goodness; the perversion of love is black sin. In the wild and agonised speeches of the Nunnery scene Hamlet cried out on marriage and honest love; in the play-scene there is little crying out, since he 'must be idle'; but we can see what has taken the place, in his mind, of love and healthfulness: lewdness and a cruel indecency. Moreover, between the two scenes, to make his meaning still more clear, Shakespeare has placed that despairing comparison of Ophelia's between the Hamlet that was and the Hamlet that is; the present Hamlet is torture to her. The 'contagious blastments' have nearly finished their work. She lacks only one more blow to lose her mind and life altogether, and that comes, in the death of the beloved father who had played his part in destroying her love. Again we may notice a significant parallel; she is driven mad, and he goes 'mad'. What has destroyed this sane and healthy love is the whole corrupt situation, working on their characters and actions. . . .

Shakespeare is determined that no peaceful radiance shall play over the consummation of Ophelia's tragedy. Here, where corruption and evil reign, nothing peaceful or radiant is possible.

This impression is deepened by the wild and grim scene that follows. When last we saw Hamlet and Laertes together it was in the Room of State; now they meet again, the brother and the lover, to struggle desperately and incoherently over Ophelia's body. This it is to which love and brotherly affection and friendship have been brought.

We may notice finally how Shakespeare completes the structure and sense of the scene, and of this whole aspect of the tragedy, by the presence of Gertrude.

Sweets to the sweet, farewell.

I hoped thou shouldst have been my Hamlet's wife;

I hoped thy bride-bed to have decked, sweet maid,

And not have strewed thy grave.

As we have remarked before, it is a tragic speech. But we know—and Gertrude seems to suspect—what it is that has blasted these fair hopes:

I doubt it is no other but the main,

His father's death, and our o'erhasty marriage.

That caused Hamlet's 'madness'; that is the ultimate cause of Ophelia's death. It was Gertrude who, yielding to the 'shameful lust' of Claudius, contributed to this manifold ruin more than anyone, except Claudius. It was her act that twisted his mind from love to obscenity:

Such an act

That blurs the grace and blush of modesty,

Calls virtue hypocrite, takes off the rose

From the fair forehead of an innocent love

And sets a blister there.

Now, broken-hearted, she laments the outcome. The scene is very nearly the consummation of Gertrude's tragedy, as well as of Ophelia's. She yielded to the King; it only remains for her to drink the King's poison.

Corruption Destroys
a Generation

Margreta de Grazia

Margreta de Grazia is the Rosenberg Professor of Humanities at the University of Pennsylvania. She has written many articles on Shakespeare and the books Shakespeare Verbatim: The Reproduction of Authenticity and the 1790 Apparatus *and* "Hamlet" Without Hamlet.

In this selection de Grazia explores how the declining, ruling generation perverts a natural order by destroying the younger generation in Denmark, as well as the country itself. Corruption has led in the end to the death of Prince Hamlet and the death of the state of Denmark on the same day. What causes things to go awry, de Grazia maintains, is a disruption in the cultural plan in that Hamlet's father's throne does not pass to the next, new generation in the person of Hamlet, but remains stuck in the older generation. Throughout, members of the younger generation are victims. In not being able to take their places as heirs, they slip out of the control of the older rulers.

In the graveyard, Hamlet incognito makes small talk with the sexton, Goodman Delver, "How long hast thou been grave-maker?" When Delver answers, Hamlet feigns ignorance of what "every fool can tell", at least every fool in Denmark: when it was that "our last King Hamlet o'ercame Fortinbras". That day, it can be assumed from the sexton's response, featured an event of such national import that time could be popularly measured from its occurrence. Only an ignoramus or an outsider would require a gloss. But for the sake of the audience, at the very start of the play, one has been intro-

Margreta de Grazia, *Hamlet Without Hamlet*. New York: Cambridge University Press, 2007. Copyright © Margreta De Grazia 2007. Reprinted with the permission of Cambridge University Press and the author.

duced. To explain Denmark's sudden military preparations, Horatio dredges up past history: Norway is threatening attack in order to recover lands King Fortinbras lost in combat with King Hamlet. Another crisis also seems at this early point to relate back to that event. The ghost of the man who "was and is the question of these wars" appears, wearing "the very armour he had on, / When he th'ambitious Norway combated", as if ready to fight once again for those same lands.

In the graveyard, when Hamlet, playing the fool or foreigner, professes not to know how long ago this epochal event occurred, Delver gives him another benchmark: "It was that very day that young Hamlet was born." . . .

What Was Meant to Be

On the very day that Denmark won these inheritable lands, a prince to inherit them was born. Like a happy astrological convergence, the coincidence seems prophetic: Hamlet was born to rule. . . .

What began long ago, in the defeat of Norway and the birth of the Danish prince, ends in the triumph of Norway and the death of the Danish prince. At the play's start, the time looked good for invading Denmark: after the sudden death of King Hamlet, the state appeared "disjoint and out of frame" (1.2.20). At the play's end, the time looks better still: the royal family has been wiped out; Denmark has collapsed. . . . During that thirty-year stretch, Denmark was maintaining its supremacy, Hamlet preparing to come into his own, and the grave-maker numbering the days of both kingdom and prince. At its end, Denmark has fallen, Hamlet is dead. . . .

The Short-Changing of the New Generation

While *Hamlet* begins shortly after the sudden death of a king and father, no generational turn takes place: Hamlet II does not succeed Hamlet I. The play's earliest audiences might well have been surprised to find that kingship had passed to the king's brother rather than his son and name-sake. It is the brother who sits triumphantly on the throne in sumptuous regalia while the son lurks on the periphery in sullen black. It is time for Hamlet to rule but it is Claudius who is made king. It is time for Hamlet to marry, in consultation with "the voice and yielding of that body / Whereof he is the head", but it is Claudius who weds with the approval of the "better wisdoms" of the Council, "For all, our thanks". Elevated to the throne by the electorate and fastened to it by his marriage to the Queen, Claudius has preempted the heir-presumptive. That he has, in the eyes of the court and state, done so legally in no way lessens the blow, for Hamlet had every reason to expect to succeed his father. . . .

At court, Hamlet's inappropriate black garb at his mother's marriage is taken to signify his continuing grief for his father's death. The King attempts to reason him out of his "obstinate condolement" by stressing the inevitability of the loss—"But you must know your father lost a father, / That father lost, lost his"—and then by offering himself as surrogate.

> [T]hink of us
>
> As of a father, for let the world take note
>
> You are the most immediate to our throne,
>
> And with no less nobility of love
>
> Than that which dearest father bears his son
>
> Do I impart toward you.

Yet Hamlet's expectation renders Claudius' attempt to cheer him sharply ironic. Offered as consolation, the proclamation can only gall. The last thing Hamlet would want is another father, an imposition that would force him back to the position of son. . . .

Disrupting the Law of Succession

Hamlet has reason to grieve inordinately, for he has lost more than a father. "Thou know'st 'tis common," the Queen intones, and Hamlet concurs, "Ay, madam, it is common". While it is common for sons to suffer the death of fathers, it is decidedly *un*common for an only son to inherit nothing of his deceased father's estate. Common law . . . protected the right of the firstborn son to inherit his father's property. The . . . law of succession depended upon the same principle of lineal descent, so that the kingdom was to descend to the issue of the king, male over female, by primogeniture. . . . With parliament's vote behind him, Claudius is the legitimate king; as far as is known at court, he has committed no legal offense in ascending to the throne. The great historian of the common law, William Blackstone, was the first to insist that Claudius obtained the kingship by due process. Hamlet, he maintains, charges Claudius of being many things during the course of the play, "drunkard, murderer, and villain, one who has carried the election by low and mean practices . . . but never hints at his being an *usurper*." . . .

In the rival empire of Norway, the king's brother instead of his son has also ascended to the throne, but without generational upset. Thirty years ago, the death of Fortinbras I apparently put his brother on the throne, Fortinbras II being then still in his minority. A generation later, the heir-apparent is ready to assume the throne, just at the point when his uncle's powers are waning. . . .

In Polonius' family, too, the son seems keen to slip out from parental control. As Fortinbras, unbeknownst to his uncle, plans to attack Denmark, as Hamlet wishes to return to Wittenberg, a wish "most retrograde" to his stepfather's and mother's desire, so Laertes determines to go to Paris, despite his father's objections. . . .

Devolution from One Generation to the Next

Thirty years marks not a point in Hamlet's lifetime, after twenty-nine and before thirty-one, but rather the endpoint of a generational cycle. The play is structured to dramatize the devolution from one generation to the next. Three father-son units are poised at the generational brink, each son scheduled to supersede his father. The older generation is clearly failing: the king in the Mousetrap is on his last legs; Norway is reported bedrid; Polonius shows signs of incipient senility. Even the play's incidentals mark volatility at the generational divide. When the touring company arrives in Elsinore, Hamlet notes how both tiers of Players are about to move up a notch. Hamlet's "old friend", now bearded, will soon graduate from adult to old men's parts; the boy, now taller and his voice about to crack, will shortly outgrow ladies' parts. The Players have been ousted from the city, to the detriment of both their reputation and profit, by a rival acting company of boys, an "eyrie of children, little eyases"; "What are they children?" Yet, as Hamlet notes, while at present "the boys carry it away," in time they will grow into the adults they now outface: "their writers do them wrong, to make them exclaim against their own succession". . . .

Ophelia Kept Childlike

The play allows Ophelia no mind of her own; instead it has her minding her father's precepts. His warnings take the place of thought. Perhaps this is why she seems to draw a blank when called upon to think. When Polonius asks her about Hamlet's professions of love, she responds, "I do not know, my Lord, what I should think". And her father tells her what to think: "Marry, I will teach you. Think yourself a baby". Her brother also tells her. Hamlet's affection, he warns, is short-lived: "The perfume and suppliance of a minute, / No more". "No more but so?" she queries. "Think it no more," he replies.

That precepts may indeed be doing the work of thought is also suggested when Hamlet, preparing to settle in for the Mousetrap play, asks if he can lie in her lap. "No, my lord", she snaps, as if he had just implored "unholy suits". He clarifies his meaning, "I mean, my head upon your lap", and asks her to clarify hers, "Do you think I meant country matters?". "I think nothing" she demurs, literally disclaiming thought of any stripe. . . .

Ophelia has lost her mind: the faculty that distinguishes human beings from both superficial pictures and irrational beasts. One thing is clear to her auditors, however: whatever she is saying, it relates to her father: "She speaks much of her father"; "Conceit upon her father"; "it springs / All from her father's death". When Laertes first sees her in this state, he, too, makes the connection, "O Rose of May" (she is now an open blossom rather than a tight bud or "button"), "is't possible a young maid's wits should be as mortal as an old man's life?" . . .

Like his sister, Laertes has a hard time minding his father's precepts after his ignominious death; and like her, too, he falls apart. He and his sister divide between them the two dramatic strains of *madness*. Ophelia is insane, Laertes enraged. . . .

Men and Women Disposed

In this play, women as well as men are generationally disposed. A generation—whether it be termed "forty years," "thirty years," "three and twenty years," or "a dozen years"— has come full circle since the time of that momentous day in Denmark's imperial history. The young, both male and female, are positioned to take over from their elders. Ophelia comes of age, but no sooner does the bud open—"O rose of May"—than it is blasted. Laertes, on the brink of coming into his own, is disentitled by his father's dishonorable death. The young fail to advance in the place of the old. Instead, Denmark's ruling dynasty is extinguished. This is what it means that weeds rather than flowers are growing in the garden of Denmark. The flowery bank is the fantasy representation of the state. The reality is less wholesome. An "unweeded garden" or "sterile promontory", Denmark more closely resembles another bank, the "Lethe wharfe" where "the fat weed" "roots" and "rots". "The Poisoner" in the Mousetrap play culls a "mixture rank, of midnight weeds" from such a lethal bank, and from that gathering is extracted the "juice of cursed hebenon", the equivalent of the "leperous distilment" poured by Claudius into his brother's ear. The source for the fatal unction Laertes contributes to Claudius' scheme derives from both *mound* and *bank*, the "mountebank" who provides a weedy "mixture" so deadly that there is no antidote for even the slightest dram:

> no cataplasm so rare,
>
> Collected from all simples that have virtue
>
> Under the moon, can save the thing from death
>
> That is but scratch'd withal.

With this "unction", the sword is anointed and the cup laced. Distillations of the fatal weeds turn out to be the bane of Denmark. They poison King Hamlet (in narrative and then in its two dramatic reenactments), the Queen ("The drink, the drink / I am poison'd,"), Claudius ("The point envenom'd too! Then, venom, to thy work"; "Drink of this potion,"), Laertes ("I am justly kill'd with mine own treachery,"), and finally Hamlet is wounded fatally with the "[u]nbated and envenom'd" sword; "No medicine in the world can do thee good".

Corruption in the Twenty-first Century

Corruption Creates Economic Inequality

Daniel Brook

Daniel Brook is a journalist whose writing has appeared in Harper's, Dissent, The San Francisco Chronicle, *and* The Boston Globe, *among other publications. Brook was a finalist in the 2003 Livingston Awards for Young Journalists and won the 2000* Rolling Stone College Journalist Competition *while a student at Yale. He lives in Philadelphia. He is the author of* The Trap: Selling Out to Stay Afloat in Winner-Take-All America.

Corruption in the crashing financial world made alarming headlines on a daily basis in 2009. But as early as 2007, when financial markets were on a roll, David Cay Johnston pointed out important signs of the greed and corruption that had created a vast economic inequality in American society in his book Free Lunch. *Brook, the author of this viewpoint, reviews this title along with Michael J. Thompson's* The Politics of Inequality. *Both of these books illustrate how the tiny majority of the wealthy have managed to grab a much larger slice of the American pie than all the rest of Americans put together. Brook explores the link between economic inequality and corruption in this article from* The Nation.

In 2006 two economists turned their critical faculties on a surprising phenomenon: diplomatic parking tickets in New York City. The pair found remarkable variation among the diplomatic corps of different countries. Kuwait's UN delegation led the pack, racking up an astounding 246 tickets per diplomat between 1997 and 2002. At the other end of the spectrum, Denmark's diplomats didn't get a single ticket. The economists discerned that the number of parking tickets per delegation tracked with Transparency International's corruption index. Diplomats from high-corruption countries like Kuwait got loads of tickets; those from low-corruption countries like, Denmark got few or none.

The Link Between Economic Inequality and Corruption

What the economists failed to note is that corruption itself tracks with another phenomenon—a nation's level of economic inequality. Dramatically unequal countries like Kuwait tend to be hideously corrupt. Countries like Denmark—by most measures, the most economically egalitarian country in the world—tend to be honest and transparent. Because of the principle of diplomatic immunity, even the careless Kuwaitis were not technically breaking any laws. Still, their parking violations speak volumes about their sense of social cohesion, or what strangers owe one another as members of civil society.

It's this type of elite misbehavior—self-serving though not always technically illegal—to which David Cay Johnston turns in *Free Lunch*. Johnston is a Pulitzer Prize-winning tax reporter at the *New York Times*. His recent articles have exposed the gaping economic inequality of George W. Bush's America and given the lie to the apologists' explanation that the new inequality stems from globalization or increasing returns to education. His analysis of tax data, which he recapitulates in *Free Lunch*, shows that it is not merely the poor and middle class who are being left behind. Even those Americans in the ninety-fifth and ninety-ninth percentiles on the income scale haven't received outsized economic benefits over the past twenty-five years. The only people leaping ahead in winner-take-all America are in the top 1 percent—and more specifically the top .1 and .01 percents. In a sense, it's not surprising to see Johnston's work in the *Times*. Even its well-educated readership is just treading water in this economy. The big winners read the *Wall Street Journal.*

Johnston's contention is an audacious one: the level of inequality and corruption in contemporary America puts us in league not with our putative economic peers, Canada, Europe and Japan, but with Brazil, Mexico and Russia, countries "in which adults have the right to vote, but real political power is wielded by a relatively narrow, and rich, segment of the population." And, as in these unequal "democracies," American elites routinely raid the public purse rather than rely on the free market to succeed. Since the "Reagan revolution," and under the guise of privatization, deregulation and "market-based solutions," wealthy interests have set up a system that Johnston dubs "corporate socialism," in which they succeed through monopoly, public subsidy and even outright theft rather than through competition. And this rigged system, Johnston argues, is what's driving the new inequality off the charts. "Subsidy economics," he writes, "is at the core of the economic malaise felt for so long by a majority of Americans."

Early in *Free Lunch*, Johnston's lumping of the United States with Brazil, Mexico and Russia sounds inflammatory, even irresponsible, but the more one reads of his litany of plutocratic shenanigans, the less far-fetched it sounds. Johnston's story of an oligarch getting $100 million in corporate welfare to open a call center filled with dead-end jobs in a frozen postindustrial city and then getting laudatory coverage in the local paper, which said oligarch owns, sounds right out of Putin's Russia. But the Frost Belt city isn't Vladivostok, and the oligarch isn't Boris Berezovsky—it's Buffalo and Warren Buffett.

As an investigative reporter, Johnston is a big-game hunter. He skewers popular plutocrats like Buffett, digs up the dirt on the unsavory sources of Paris Hilton's fortune and details Apple executive Steve Jobs's backdated stock options thievery. Some of these stories are well-known—Enron's market manipulation, for example—but Johnston's reporting makes the outrage boil over anyway. Unfortunately, the outrage sends Johnston's prose into overdrive. His description of "government giveaways [that] flourish like weeds on Miracle-Gro" makes you wish he'd shown his copy to some strait-laced editors at the *Times* or even stuck with the standard cliché, "pop up like mushrooms."

It is Johnston's investigative skills, however, that distinguish the book from the usual social critic's rant. He does his homework, crunches the numbers and makes astonishing discoveries. For example, the sporting goods chain Cabela's, a leading purveyor of hunting equipment (and Dick Cheney's favorite place to shop), earned $223.4 million in profits between 2004 and 2006 while soaking up at least $293.7 million in subsidies on its Nebraska stores alone. Playing one small town against another, Cabela's arranged deals to waive property taxes, let the company pocket sales taxes and even get free land for its stores and distribution centers. In a very real sense, Johnston shows, Cabela's is in the corporate welfare business, not the sporting goods business.

Johnston also profiles a mom-and-pop sporting goods store in tiny Hamburg, Pennsylvania, put out of business when a Cabela's comes to town. The reporting is vivid, but the analysis is weak. This is indeed a case of unfair competition, but Johnston argues that in a system of fair competition, mom-and-pop stores would do just fine. A dogged reporter, he's dug up a case of a mom-and-pop that can beat the big chain on price. But is such a comparison typical? There are plenty of reasons to oppose the big-box behemoths, but high prices is rarely one of them. With their economies of scale, chains can usually undercut independent stores without resorting to corporate welfare.

So Johnston ends up arguing, in effect, that laissez faire would be fair. But would it? He repeatedly makes references to how much Adam Smith would object if he could see our system, where "corporate socialists" troll Washington and the state capitols for favors rather than competing on the open market. Perhaps this is purely rhetorical—a way to appeal to a country where Smith is arguably more revered than the actual founders of the country. But is objecting to plutocracy in America on the grounds that it's not Smithian really the most effective way to combat the new inequality? And is crony capitalism really the main source of the new inequality? It's true that American crony capitalism produces even more inequality than a Smithian laissez-faire system would. But Smith's laissez faire would still concentrate money in the hands of a few. That's what unregulated capitalism does. The new inequality is the result both of market-based reforms that are implemented honestly and those implemented dishonestly.

Johnston seems to believe that our country is becoming unequal because it is corrupt, not that it is becoming corrupt because it is unequal. Certainly corruption and inequality are mutually reinforcing phenomena, but the causation generally runs from inequality to corruption. Rather than conjure up a Johnstonian metaphor here, let's just say he's putting the cart before the horse.

The Gap Between Rich and Poor

In a sense, Johnston's book is exactly the type of angry but ultimately ineffectual analysis that Michael Thompson, an assistant professor at William Paterson University, takes aim at in *The Politics of Inequality*. Why, Thompson asks, is the critique of inequality—so salient for the first 200 years of American history—falling flat today, when inequality is as bad as it's ever been? To take on the new inequality; Thompson argues, we must rediscover the older tradition of critiquing inequality from a small-r republican perspective. In this line of thinking, the problem with inequality is not so much that it is unfair for so few to have so much while so many have so little, or even that inequality undermines formal democratic politics.

Rather, it's that high degrees of economic inequality under-
mine democratic society itself, the society of equals. "Western
political thought, from the writings of Plato on through those
of John Dewey, saw economic inequality as dangerous . . . not
out of a liberal concern for 'fairness' or opportunity but because it marked divisions that threatened a culture of equality
and freedom," Thompson writes. Thus, when Supreme Court
Justice Louis Brandeis reputedly warned, "We can have a democracy in this country or we can have great wealth concentrated in the hands of the few. We cannot have both," he was
not offering an opinion. He was stating a fact. We can be a republic or we can be a society where elites park in front of the
fire hydrants.

Ever since the beginnings of democracy Thompson explains, political thinkers have understood that a democratic
society can not endure under conditions of extreme inequality. There was broad agreement on this principle. The difference between left and right was not that progressive thinkers
opposed extreme inequality and conservative theorists supported it. Rather, left and right differed only on why they
feared inequality. Left thinkers worried that in a system of extreme inequality; the conspiratorial rich would subvert the
forms of democracy for their own self-interested ends. You
can hear this fear in Thomas Jefferson's warning that "I hope
we shall crush in its birth the aristocracy of our moneyed corporations which dare already to challenge our government."
Right-leaning thinkers worried that extreme inequality would
push the poor to rise up and lead to mob rule—John Adams's
fear of the "lawless, tyrannical rabble." Centrists like Aristotle
were equally fearful of rich and poor. The Athenian philosopher thought that under unequal economic conditions, the
poor view the system as a conspiracy against them and see no
reason to follow the rules; similarly, the rich come to feel that
they are better than their fellow citizens and see themselves as
above the law. The key to a stable republic, Aristotle dis-

cerned, is a large and stable middle class. This understanding was hardly limited to philosophical idealists flitting about in Aristophanes' *Clouds*. Even Machiavelli, the consummate pragmatist, not known for his sentimental attachments to abstract ideals, argued that a republic could endure only under conditions of relative economic equality; otherwise, corruption or revolution would ensue.

Economic Inequality and Democracy

For 2,000 years, hardly anyone thought extreme inequality was tenable in a republic. So while William Greider has described (in these pages) the New Right agenda as "rolling back the twentieth century," it is even more audacious than that—it is to roll back Western civilization (or perhaps human civilization, period, for even Confucius warned, "Where wealth is centralized, the people are dispersed. Where wealth is distributed, the people are brought together"). While Aristotle began Western political thought with his insight that "man is by nature a political animal," Margaret Thatcher sought to end it: "Who is society? There is no such thing! There are individual men and women and there are families."

Admittedly, in American political thought there has always been a counterargument that high degrees of economic inequality, if established under conditions of open competition, could coexist with democracy. Thompson traces this tradition from Alexander Hamilton through John C. Calhoun to Milton Friedman. But none of these thinkers, so sanguine about the risks inequality poses to democracy, were particularly committed to democracy. Hamilton humiliated himself on the floor of the Constitutional Convention by arguing that what the new nation really needed was a "monarch"; Calhoun was America's leading intellectual apologist for slavery; Milton Friedman advised Chilean dictator Gen. Augusto Pinochet. The only thinkers who dismiss extreme inequality as no threat to democratic society appear to be, at best, indifferent to democracy.

Considering the brevity of Thompson's sketches—Plato is discussed in six pages, Machiavelli in one—academics may dismiss the book as drive-by intellectual history. But if anything, the book is not broad enough. Why limit discussion to political philosophers simply because a balkanized academy calls for it? Why not analyze political rhetoric—the free-labor ideology of Lincoln's Republican Party, for example—and religious thought? To what extent is our embrace of inequality rooted in our Puritan forebears' transformation of the religion of Jesus, in which worldly wealth was a barrier to salvation ("It is easier for a camel to go through the eye of a needle than for a rich man to enter the kingdom of God") for a faith in which worldly wealth was a sign of salvation?

How, after 2,000 years of broad agreement that extreme levels of economic inequality were anathema to self-rule, does one explain the United States, an ostensibly democratic country where the concentration of wealth exceeds not only those of our peer countries but that of imperial Rome? Thompson blames this on the triumph of liberalism, with its emphasis on individual rights anti equal opportunity, over republicanism, with its emphasis on civic virtue, social equality and the absence of domination. Conventionally seen as being in tension, liberalism and republicanism, Thompson argues, were initially aligned in their opposition to feudalism. Early American liberals assumed that an economy of open competition would lead to reasonable levels of economic equality. After all, every person had the capacity to work; freed from the constraints of feudalism, each worker could keep the fruits of his labor.

In the early American economy of small farms and shops, this idea seemed reasonable. What liberals didn't understand was that in the industrial economy of large corporations that would develop after the Civil War, work and reward would again be separated. In the feudal system, serfs worked land owned by nobles; nobles got rich while serfs remained poor. Under industrial capitalism, workers work in corporations owned by industrialists and shareholders, who similarly get rich while workers often get shortchanged. Blind-sided by the rise of industrial capitalism, with its bifurcation of work and reward, liberalism was impotent to take on the inequality of the first Gilded Age or its re-emergence in the second Gilded Age today. While a liberal ideology of open competition has been able to take on racial and gender inequality, it has nothing to offer against the scourge of economic inequality. Capitalism's Smithian system of seemingly free and open competition is a mechanism for generating extreme economic inequality. Until liberals understand this—including liberals like David Cay Johnston—there is little chance of rolling back the new inequality.

Consequences of Economic Inequality

Thompson urges broader criticism of inequality than analysis of the economic gains of the top 1 percent or how the rich monopolize government power. He writes of the "decline of civic engagement, the erosion of political life, and the shattering of a once vibrant public sphere" that ensues under conditions of extreme inequality. At its best moments, *Free Lunch* explores these themes, as when Johnston describes the fate of urban park systems under privatization. (In Los Angeles, where user fees have replaced tax funding, parks in poor neighborhoods rot while those in posh areas shine.) Thompson's book is not a work of reporting, but the quotes he unearths from thinkers describing unequal societies of times past do seem to offer glimpses of our own time. Matthew Arnold's description of a Dickensian England in which extreme inequality is "materializing our upper class, vulgarizing our middle class, and brutalizing our lower class" certainly sounds prescient. "This is to fail in civilization," Arnold concludes. And when Thompson quotes Montesquieu as saying, "In monarchies and despotic governments, nobody aims at equality . . . they all aspire to superiority. People of the very lowest condition desire to emerge from their obscurity only to lord it over their fellow-subjects," you can't help but think of the French baron in powdered wig and tights, notebook in hand, wandering the streets of Las Vegas, past casinos and pawn shops.

Though Thompson provides a great service in revisiting—and reviving—the tradition of seeing extreme economic inequality and democracy as incompatible, the Montesquieu quote raises a dark truth the author never fully confronts. While it would be comforting to assume that extreme inequality would naturally lead to popular demands for greater equality, in highly unequal societies, people often aspire not to roll back inequality but to benefit from it. How to turn a nation of gamblers into a nation of citizens is the question that looms over America.

Corruption in a Global Corporate Empire

Paul Kingsnorth

Paul Kingsnorth is a writer, environmentalist, and poet. He has written for publications worldwide.

In the following viewpoint, Kingsnorth reviews John Perkins's nonfiction work Confessions of an Economic Hit Man. *Perkins describes himself as an EHM, an Economic Hit Man, whose job it was to use any unscrupulous means to influence politics in other countries to enrich international corporations, particularly a firm called Chas. T. Main, Inc. (which he refers to as Main). While the idea of widespread corruption is unnerving, the good news is that more and more people are becoming aware of the great danger generated by this corruption. Kingsnorth argues that we can only dismantle the empire of these corporations when we really understand how they function—which Perkins helps us to do with his informative book.*

I'll bet that, you have at some stage used the word "empire" to refer to the world dominance of the United States. You may have used it in connection with the war on Iraq, or the US-led project of economic globalisation. It is also quite likely that you have been scoffed at by someone for using the term, been painted as a naive old lefty who doesn't understand the subtleties of politics and power. If so, John Perkins is here to show that you were right all along—and that, if anything, you were probably understating the case.

Confessions of an Economic Hit Man

Confessions of an Economic Hit Man, Perkins's painfully honest autobiography, is one of the most remarkable books I have read in a long time. It is also one of the most frightening.

From 1971 to 1981, Perkins was employed as an EHM (ie, "economic hit man") whose role is to "cheat countries around the globe out of trillions of dollars. Their tools include fraudulent financial reports, rigged elections, pay-offs, extortion, sex and murder. They play a game as old as empire, but one that has taken on terrifying dimensions during this time of globalisation." It sounds more like the cover blurb for a John le Carre thriller than a work of non-fiction—and indeed, Perkins tells us that his publisher initially suggested he fictionalise the book, as no one would believe it otherwise.

His story begins when, as a young graduate, he is approached by an international consulting firm called Main and offered a job as an economist. He soon finds out what the work entails.

There were two primary objectives of my work. First I was to justify huge international loans that would funnel money to Main and other US companies (such as Bechtel, Halliburton, Stone & Webster and Brown & Root) through massive engineering and construction projects. Second, I would work to bankrupt the countries that received those loans ... so they would be for ever beholden to their creditors, and so they would present easy targets when we [the US] needed favours, including military bases, UN votes or access to oil and other natural resources.

There, in a paragraph, is your recipe for empire, and over the course of a decade, Perkins helped build it.

The Start of an Empire

He started in Indonesia, where his task was to plan an electricity grid for Java. He was instructed to produce wildly inflated economic growth forecasts that would allow international banks and USAID [United States Agency for International Development] to justify vast loans to the Indonesians, which their government would be unable to pay back, creating dependency on the US.

He did well, and was sent on to Panama to do the same thing for its "master development plan", under which the

World Bank would invest billions in the country's infrastructure, sell the construction rights to US corporations and, as Main hoped, force an anti-American government to climb down over its ambitions to take back control of the Panama Canal.

Then it was on to Saudi Arabia, which provides perhaps the most shocking story of all. There, Perkins was required not simply to produce the usual inflated growth forecasts to justify loans and corporate contracts, but to "find ways that would ensure that a large portion of petrodollars found their way back to the United States". America needed dependable supplies of oil; there was to be no repeat of the OPEC-led [Organization of the Petroleum Exporting Countries] 1970s oil crisis that nearly bankrupted its economy.

Disbanding the Empire

Perkins did his masters proud with a plan that made Saudi Arabia "the cow we can milk until the sun sets on our retirement". The Saudi government agreed to maintain oil supplies and prices that would be acceptable to the US. In return, the Americans offered total political and military support. But the clincher was the desert kingdom's promise to use its petrodollars to purchase US government securities, the interest on which was to be spent "developing" the kingdom along western lines. In other words, "our own US Department of the Treasury would hire us, at Saudi expense, to build infrastructure projects and even entire cities throughout the Arabian peninsula". Genius.

At this point, it is tempting to give in to despair and stop reading, but please don't. Perkins's aim is to expose the empire in order to dismantle it. He got out, he emphasises—and the wider world can get out, too. We can disband the empire, but only if we know how it really functions. There are few better places to find out.

Corruption and the Pentagon

Pratap Chatterjee

Pratap Chatterjee, an independent investigative reporter and au-
thor, has won many awards for his work, including one from the
National Newspaper Association. He is the author of Iraq, Inc.:
A Profitable Occupation.

In this selection, Chatterjee explains the degree to which the
military has been revolutionized and exploited by one massive
corporation—Halliburton—and its many branches. The U.S.
military, under the urging and protection of then-vice president
Dick Cheney and former secretary of defense Donald Rumsfeld,
awarded billion-dollar, no-bid contracts to Halliburton to take
on noncombat work in Iraq. This work included chores that sol-
diers used to do—like preparing meals and transporting goods.
Chief executive officers and directors made fortunes from the
contracts, but the services provided were inadequate. Many Hal-
liburton staff members found it easy to line their pockets through
fraud. Further corruption stems from the fact that by far most of
their labor is done by the poorest of the poor from other Third
World countries. Chatterjee contrasts the luxurious lifestyle of
one director with the life of workers living on the edge of pov-
erty.

[A] truism has been repeated by many a general throughout history. General Matthew B. Ridgway, who helped
plan the airborne invasion of Sicily in July 1943, once said,
"What throws you in combat is rarely the fact that your tacti-
cal scheme was wrong . . . but that you failed to think through
the hard, cold facts of logistics."

Pratap Chatterjee, *Halliburton's Army. How a Well-Connected Texas Oil Company Revo-*
lutionized the Way America Makes War. Cambridge, MA: Nation Books, 2009. Copyright © 2009 Pratap Chatterjee. Reprinted by permission of Nation Books a member of
Perseus Books, L.L.C.

But what is harder yet is recruiting the people to carry out those less-glamorous tasks. In 1904, U.S. Secretary of War Elihu Root warned, "Our trouble will never be in raising soldiers. Our trouble will always be the limit of possibility in transporting, clothing, arming, feeding, and caring for our soldiers. . . ."

If JFK [President John F. Kennedy] had a hard time dispatching a draft army to do these tasks in Vietnam, George [W.] Bush faced a far tougher task convincing twenty-first-century U.S. teenagers to volunteer to peel potatoes, dig ditches and clean toilets in the desert for months, even years, at a stretch.

Outsourcing

Complicating matters further was the fact that Secretary of Defense Donald Rumsfeld asked General Tommy Franks to draw up plans for a small force that would use "shock and awe" for the invasion of Iraq, rather than the five hundred thousand troops that Franks estimated would be needed for a conventional war. Likewise, in February 2003, when army chief of staff General Eric Shinseki publicly stated that several hundred thousand troops would be needed to sustain an occupation, he was rebuked by Rumsfeld's deputy, Paul Wolfowitz.

So Franks followed up on Rumsfeld's suggestion of September 10, 2001, to outsource anything that was not inherently military to contractors. Paul Cerjan, then director of Halliburton/KBR's worldwide military logistics operation, explained what was outsourced and why in a *Frontline* interview, "I would put it in terms of what used to be a three-tier definition for military forces. One was combat forces—infantry, armor, artillery, and such; one's combat support forces, which essentially were MPs [military police] and other activities that supported the war fighter; and then the third one is combat service support forces, which is the tails. And so the tail lends itself to contracting; there's no question about it. It's a mission-critical function when you're supplying food for troops. Without full bellies, they can't fight."

Globalization made it easy to find migrant labor to do this work even during a dangerous and unpopular war. An even greater benefit of contracting out these logistical jobs was that this dedicated work force was able to go beyond the traditional army chow to provide a dazzling array of creature comforts that convinced reluctant U.S. soldiers to continue to sign up to fight in Iraq—from all-you-can-eat dinner buffets to Burger King and Pizza Hut on demand, as well as hot showers and an endless supply of video games—mimicking their lifestyles back at home, except that in Iraq, the soldiers didn't even have to clean up after themselves.

Contrasting Lines of CEOs and Workers

The Fahaheel Expressway shoots like an arrow out of Kuwait's city center, bearing southeast toward Saudi Arabia, until it merges with King Faheed Bin Abdul Aziz road on the way to Camp Arifjan, which is the biggest U.S. military base in Kuwait. A modern, six-lane highway that was completed more than a decade ago, the highway connects to the booming new neighborhoods of Fintas, Mahboula, Mangaf, and Fahaheel that together make up a spanking new city that rivals the country's somewhat old and decrepit capital. . . .

If you wander through the unpaved dusty backstreets of Mahboula, you will run into thousands of Egyptians, Fijians, Indians, Filipinos, and U.S. citizens who are flocking to live in the small apartments that make up the highrise residential complexes that are growing like mushrooms around the area. What draws them are the jobs on the military bases like Camp Arifjan, as well as the new refineries and related industries planned. KBR and PWC are household names here, as are a host of other U.S. military contractors like CSA, IAP, and ITT.

A sign reading "War Profiteering Is Wrong" is held high during a protest at the annual Halliburton shareholders' meeting in Duncan, Oklahoma, in 2006. The corruption that permeates Hamlet *can be seen in many corporations and governments around the world.* AP Images.

Not far from Mahboula is Mangaf, where the wealthy executives of KBR make their home at the Hilton. It is here that Tom Crum, KBR's chief operating officer, once demanded that hotel staff get his wife a diamond-encrusted Cartier watch in the middle of the night, when hers mysteriously disappeared. ("Get off your f&^%ing ass, put my wife in a car, and go get her a watch," Crum is alleged to have told Camille Geha, the Egyptian sales manager at the Hilton in Kuwait, in early 2004. Aware that the company was spending up to millions at the hotel, Geha is said to have told an unnamed hotel worker to have a jewelry store at the Marina Mall down the road opened in the middle of the night to get a new watch.). . .

Profits

In mid-July 2008, David Lesar owned 961,003 shares in Halliburton, worth just shy of $50 million. Over the last few years, Lesar has sold more than half a million shares, collecting tens of millions in cash—indeed, at one point his holdings in the company were valued at $129.4 million (in early September 2005, shortly after Hurricane Katrina hit). Factoring in his stock options, *Forbes* magazine's April 2008 CEO compensation report calculated that Lesar made an average of $20 million a year over the last five years.

There is no doubt that this astronomical salary is linked to the company's soaring revenues.... In 2004 the company generated $75 million in profits, swelling to $172 million in 2005 on revenues of $5.4 billion, dropping slightly to $166 million in 2006. The company's share price has also risen exponentially from a low of $4.98 on January 18, 2002 (it was $14.36 on September 10, 2001).... Halliburton's share price has inched upward until it hit $32.51 on the day it finally spun off KBR in mid-April 2007 (which was effectively worth $65.02 as the company had created a two-for-one stock split). By July 2008, Halliburton's stock price had reached $50 a share (or $100 for the original shares), reflecting the boom in oil prices. KBR's shares were stuck at a respectable $30 (up from the $21 when they were first issued in November 2006)....

Halliburton/KBR continues to win major government contracts. When Hurricane Katrina hit the Gulf Coast in August 2005, Halliburton/KBR was tasked with the reconstruction of several naval stations and the Stennis Space Center on the Mississippi/Louisiana border. "Due to the magnitude of Hurricane Katrina and the urgent requirements for emergency response, the corps was authorized to tap into the existing contracts of sister services," said Army Corps [of Engineers] spokesperson Carol Sanders. The main contracting vehicle used was CONCAP (Construction Capabilities), issued by the Naval Facilities Engineering Command, the very same contract used to build prisons in Guantánamo Bay, Cuba. Under this navy contract, Halliburton/KBR was also awarded an early contract to pump water from Plaquemines Parish in Louisiana and set up a temporary morgue, which is not normally a military job.

In January 2006, the Army Corps awarded the company a contract worth up to $385 million to build temporary detention centers in the event of an immigration crisis at the border. . . .

The Losers: Taxpayers

Tales of fraud and abuse worth millions of dollars of taxpayer money in the Halliburton/KBR contract started to surface within a few months of the 2003 invasion. Whistle-blowers came forward to report allegations of overcharges for everything from towels to trucks while internal Pentagon numbers presented by Congressman Henry Waxman suggested that billions of dollars worth of invoices could be missing.

The slew of investigations that have been detailed in the previous chapters suggests that at the very least, the company was simply not prepared to set up for anything on the scale of the job General Tommy Franks handed them in 2003. Marie deYoung told a Senate Democratic Policy Committee hearing that even the company's "manual accounting system" was obsolete, despite the fact that she says that there was "no reason in the world why Halliburton can't do real time data management." . . .

Lax oversight at Halliburton/KBR allowed some procurement staff to take advantage of the situation. Whistle-blowers have testified that Halliburton supervisors routinely announced, "Don't worry about price. It's cost-plus." This in turn encouraged fleet managers to import unnecessary quantities of expensive vehicles, and companies like Altanmia and managers like Jeff Mazon to charge several times the going rate for fuel.

If that wasn't bad enough, as the disaster in the Iraqi oilfields indicates, Halliburton/KBR also failed in certain crucial areas despite its technological expertise, because of the lack of independence and oversight. A Pentagon order to fix broken pipelines with bad technology simply wasn't possible just because the order was issued. A system of checks and balances could have allowed experienced engineers to veto bad plans and suggest alternatives that would have solved that matter quicker and more cheaply.

Halliburton/KBR officials wave away these allegations of fraud and abuse as either inaccurate or the normal cost of doing business. When I brought the allegations of waste, fraud, and abuse up with David Lesar, Halliburton CEO, at the company's annual meeting in 2006 and asked him what he had to say about the canceled contracts and overcharges, he replied: "I've been to Iraq a number of times, and it's a tough place to do work. I'm proud of our folks there and . . . we will continue to support the troops. I think we're just going to respectfully disagree with each other on the rest of your comments." . . .

Labor Exploitation

One major argument that military officials make is that outsourcing should be cheaper—and it rings true. "[It's] not immediately evident to somebody listening to you because they're going to see that a truck driver, for instance, who is brought over here from the States [is] paid much more than anybody who was driving a truck for the armed services in the past was getting. How is it cheaper?" says Cerjan. "Because we increased the number of soldiers who can go out on patrol. And when you look at the cost of that soldier and a lifecycle environment, the dollars just show up. It's more cost-effective to outsource some of those activities, those functions, outside of the military. I didn't do the numbers, but I'm telling you, it's cheaper. You're paying some people more money. You're talking about expatriates who come over here. There's an American truck driver who gets more money, but you don't take into account the third-country nationals we hired at less wage because they can come over here and do it cheaper."

Titoko Savuwati, the Fijian truck driver in Kuwait, who lives basically from paycheck to paycheck, sending the bulk of his earnings back to his family in Totoya Lau, can testify to the fact that the Halliburton/KBR and PWC are saving a bundle. When I last saw Savuwati in the spring of 2008, PWC had suspended him from driving into Iraq for no apparent reason, although he guessed it was probably because of his injured foot, so his modest hazard bonus of KWD 50 (US$183) has disappeared. Making matters worse, he says that the company failed to pay him for the several months that he was in Kuwait. His bank balance was zero.

Savuwati is just one of dozens of Fijian truck drivers who claim that PWC often shortchanges them on their meager monthly salaries of KWD 175 (US$640). They have clubbed together and pooled their money to hire a local lawyer— Abdul Majeed Khuraibet, a former Kuwaiti police officer, whose office is on the sixth floor of the Al-Saleh building, opposite the Maghreb mosque in the heart of Kuwait City—to fight on their behalf. The problem is that they never bothered to keep their pay stubs, so their claims are hard to document.

"Why do these companies cheat these men?" Majeed asked me, when I interviewed him about their prospects. "They do all their dirty work and they cannot even go home."

The answer is simple: The low salaries and lack of benefits for migrant workers is one of the principal ways that Halliburton/KBR generates profits and the Pentagon and U.S. taxpayer save money. The salaries are not the only way that the Pentagon is saving money compared to previous wars; it no longer has to recruit new soldiers, pay for training (which exceeds $100,000), or pay for the benefits package that soldiers expect when they leave the military for things like college tuition, healthcare, and pensions, a package which generally adds up to tens of thousands of dollars per soldier. In extreme cases disability may be as high as $5 million.

The U.S. citizens who work as truckers and supervisors are much better off than Savuwati and are paid salaries that are much higher than the average U.S. soldier, but even they do not run up training costs or veteran benefits. Even if they worked for four years straight in Iraq, which is rare, they would still cost the taxpayer less than an ordinary recruit.

I asked the commanders I met at LSA Anaconda in Iraq and Camp Arifjan if they were worried about the low wages and lack of human rights for workers. The answer was almost always a shrug. When I brought up the many examples of petty fraud and waste, they were only mildly worried, but they pointed out that most of the examples I was citing dated back to 2004, which they claim to have resolved today. . . .

What is perhaps more disturbing is that the labor practices in Iraq are now becoming commonplace on domestic U.S. military bases. In late October 2005, federal immigration officials conducted two surprise raids at Belle Chasse Naval Base near New Orleans and processed fourteen undocumented people who worked for Halliburton/KBR subcontractors doing Hurricane Katrina reconstruction.

The National Committee of La Raza (NCLR) also found multiple abuses by Halliburton subcontractors. On November 18, 2005, NCLR staff visited a "tent city" of Latino workers in Gulfport [Mississippi]. They reported, "Workers repeatedly complained about contractors who hired them for long periods of time and then refused to pay them for their labor. For example, Esteban J., a Mexican worker who left behind a wife and four children in Veracruz, Mexico, was recruited in North Carolina by a subcontractor hired by Halliburton/KBR to perform debris removal with 105 other workers."

"The subcontractor promised an hourly wage of $13, along with food, lodging, and overtime pay; yet, after several weeks, the subcontractor had not paid any of them, and many of the men were forced to sleep outside. After making several demands, Esteban was finally paid a week's worth of wages with little for him to send back home to his family," reported NCLR. Esteban estimated that the contractor owed him two hundred hours worth of wages and consequently filed a wage-and-hour claim with the Department of Labor. The agency ruled favorably in the case and ordered Halliburton/KBR to pay $141,887 in back wages to Esteban and his fellow workers. . . .

Government Corruption and Accountability

I began . . . with the stories of Dick Cheney and Donald Rumsfeld, the two men who created Halliburton's Army of migrant labor and forged the revolution in military affairs to allow the United States to pursue its Global War on Terror. While these two men have been outspoken on "defeating terrorism," neither of them have chosen to say a word about the company in the last several years, and it may fall to the next generation of politicians, in 2009, to hold them accountable for the waste, fraud, and abuse, including human rights abuses, in executing this war. Should one want to track them down, they will probably be found in the quiet resort town of St. Michaels, on Chesapeake Bay, in Maryland, just about an hour's drive from Washington, DC.

Torture and Espionage

Democracy Now!

The nationally syndicated radio news show Democracy Now! *is hosted by journalists Amy Goodman and Juan Gonzalez.*

The following is the transcription of a radio news show on recent discussions about officials who encouraged and approved of torture in dealing with suspected terrorists. It was inspired by Vermont senator Patrick Leahy's proposal for a "Truth Commission" to investigate the Department of Justice, which may have endorsed the use of torture in violation of the U.S. Constitution and international law. The department may have also encouraged warrantless searches, suppression of free speech, and the transferring of prisoners to countries known to use torture. In short, Leahy proposed an investigation of what was done above and beyond the law. Michael Ratner, a human rights attorney, reacts to Leahy's proposal by saying that it is inadequate until it insists on prosecution of the government officials responsible. Although prosecution is still being debated in the United States, such plans are already under way in other countries.

*D*emocracy Now! Co-Host *[Juan] Gonzalez:* On Capitol Hill, debate has begun over forming a truth commission to shed light on the [George W.] Bush administration's secret polices on detention, interrogation and domestic spying. A hearing on the issue was held Wednesday [March 4, 2009], two days after the [Barack] Obama administration released a series of once-secret Bush administration Justice Department memos that authorized President Bush to deploy the military to carry out raids inside the United States. The author of the memos, John Yoo, said Bush could disregard the First and Fourth Amendments of the Constitution.

Amy Goodman, "The Case for Establishing a Truth Commission for Bush's Torture and Spying Crew," AlterNet.org, March 7, 2009. Reproduced by permission of King Features Syndicate.

Senator Leahy's "Truth Commission"

During a Senate Judiciary Committee hearing on Wednesday, committee chair Patrick Leahy said the newly released memos highlight the need for a truth commission.

Sen. Patrick Leahy Vice President Dick Cheney and others from the Bush administration continue to assert that their tactics, including torture, were appropriate and effective. I don't think we should let only one side define history on such important questions. It's important for an independent body to hear these assertions, but also for others, if we're going to make an objective and independent judgment about what happened and whether it did make our nation safe or less safe.

Just this week, the Department of Justice released more alarming documents from the Office of Legal Counsel demonstrating the last administration's pinched view of constitutionally protected rights. The memos disregarded the Fourth and First Amendment, justifying warrantless searches, the suppression of free speech, surveillance without warrants, and transferring people to countries known to conduct interrogations that violate human rights. How can anyone suggest such policies do not deserve a thorough, objective review?

I am encouraged that the Obama administration is moving forward. I'm encouraged that a number of the things that— number of the issues we've been stonewalled on before are now becoming public. But how did we get to a point where we were holding a legal US resident for more than five years in a military brig without ever bringing charges against him? How did we get to a point where Abu Ghraib [an Iraqi prison where the abuse and torture of prisoners was inflicted by U.S. Army and government personnel] happened? How did we get to a point where the United States government tried to make Guantanamo Bay a law-free zone, in order to deny accountability for our actions? How did we get to a point where our premier intelligence agency, the CIA, destroyed nearly a hundred videotapes with evidence of how detainees were being interrogated? How did we get to a point where the White House could say, "If we tell you to do it, even if it breaks the law, it's alright, because we're above the law"? . . .

Attorney Ratner's View of Accountability

[Host Amy] Goodman: Human rights attorney Michael Ratner joins us now in the firehouse studio, president of the Center for Constitutional Rights, author of the book *The Trial of Donald Rumsfeld*, among others.

Welcome to *Democracy Now!* I want to talk about the secret memos. Let's start with this hearing that has been called by Patrick Leahy, chair of the Senate Judiciary Committee, calling for an investigation into Bush administration crimes.

Michael Ratner: You know, I won't say I'm exactly biased here, but I think essentially that the Leahy commission is an excuse for non-prosecution. It's essentially saying, "Let's put some stuff on the public record. Let's immunize people. And then," as he even said, "let's turn the page and go forward." That's really an excuse for non-prosecution. And in the face of what we've seen in this country, which is essentially a coup d'etat, a presidential dictatorship and torture, it's essentially a mouse-like reaction to what we've seen. And it's being set up really by a liberal establishment that is really, in some ways, in many ways, on the same page as the establishment that actually carried out these laws. And it's saying, "OK, let's expose it, and then let's move on."

And he even says, he says what we're going to do with the truth commission is we're going to look and see what mistakes were made. I mean, just ask the hundred people who were tortured in the secret sites about what mistakes were made, or ask the 750 people at Guantanamo, or ask the people at Abu Ghraib. This is not about mistakes. This is about fundamental lawbreaking, about the disposal of the Constitution, and about the end of treaties. So I think, actually, that Leahy's current proposal is extremely dangerous. I call it the lame commission or basically an excuse for non-prosecution. . . .

Look at, there's a lot of pressure in this Country right now for prosecutions. I mean, the polls indicate that people want to see a criminal investigation. We've had open—open and notorious admissions of waterboarding by people like Cheney. And we know that waterboarding is torture, even according to Obama. . . .

Secret Memos on Torture

What we see in these memos—and I recommend them to everybody, because you read these, you are seeing essentially the legal underpinnings of a police state or a dictatorship of the president. There's no doubt about it. That's what it is, and it's not theoretical. These were the actual building blocks of what we had in this country for eight years, in which—and the one you mentioned when we opened, Juan, that what happened here was one of these memos said the military could operate in the United States, and operate in the United States despite the Posse Comitatus law, which prohibits the military from operating in the United States. And when it operates—this is really extraordinary—they can arrest and detain—"arrest" is not the right word—kidnap anyone they want and send them to a detention place anywhere in the world without any kind of law.

And then, on top of that, they can disregard the First Amendment. So this conversation we're having right now, they could say, "Well, this is harmful to the national security of the United States"—that's what these memos say—"this type of conversation is harmful, and we can ban this conversation." And then they could put the military at the door to the firehouse and come in and say the Fourth Amendment, the one that protects us against unlawful searches, that the

Protestors demonstrate a method of torture called "water boarding" on a volunteer in front of the Justice Department in Washington, D.C., in 2007. The Department of Justice may have endorsed the use of torture, which is in violation of the U.S. Constitution and international law. AP Images.

military could walk in here, search all of us and see if we have anything they don't like on us. . . .

There's another memo here on extraordinary rendition. We've discussed it here before. That's where you send people overseas for torture. You nab them or grab them in Pakistan or Afghanistan, send them to another country where it's more likely than not where they'll be tortured. And these memos go through why that may—the argument they make is that that's not against the law, that the Convention Against Torture doesn't apply and the anti-torture statute, you know, can be avoided by not having the intent to carry out torture. So they essentially authorize sending people—sending people for torture.

Then, two of the memos—and this is pretty interesting—actually concerned Jose Padilla. Jose Padilla, you remember, got off the plane in Chicago, the so-called dirty bomber, never charged with that, and when he's in the prison, the military comes to the prison door. They knock. Maybe they knock. And they say, "Give us Jose Padilla." And they grab him. This is in America. This is in the United States. And they take him, and for five years they put him in a military brig. Two of the memos justify and say the President had the power to do that to Jose Padilla, an American citizen living in the United States, that the military could come in—could come in and get him. . . .

And there's another memo on the warrantless wiretapping that essentially says the commander-in-chief can carry out warrantless wiretapping as his commander-in-chief power.

Toward Dictatorship

I have to say that . . . to see these memos, to put it into that they were actually instrumentalized—this is not just theoretical; this is what was happening here for eight years, essentially a dictatorship—and then to see the response of many of the Democrats here to saying, "Oh, let's just expose it and turn the page," I mean, what we're saying is that's the way it's going to happen again, because unless you prosecute people, there is no deterrence for not doing this again. And it's out there, it's public. If you're going to do a commission—and I'm opposed completely to the Leahy type—if you're going to do one, you can't bury the issue of prosecution. You have to appoint a special prosecutor and make sure a commission of inquiry works together, because a commission can tear up and finish up prosecutions by giving immunity.

The Man Who Wrote the Torture Memos

Gonzalez: And Michael, the prime author of these memos, John Yoo, what happened to him? He went back for awhile, left the Bush administration, went back to Berkeley, law school, to teach. What's happened with him since?

Ratner: Well, first of all, I think that these memos, these most recent ones, shred any semblance, any scintilla of reputation that John Yoo ever had that he was, you know, doing something in essentially an honest way. I mean, this finishes his reputation. I think the only—the questions we're faced with are, is he going to be disbarred, and is he going to be prosecuted?

And it's interesting. You know, two of the memos, which I didn't mention, were issued by Steven Bradbury, who was head of the office that John Yoo was formerly in, the Office of Legal Counsel [OLC]. And those memos are the—they were done within a few weeks of the Bush administration leaving office, in fact, one within a week of him leaving office, essentially, in a relatively mealy-mouthed way, saying he cautions against looking at the Yoo memos, that they shouldn't—the OLC doesn't really agree with them anymore. But he has a footnote in there saying—to protect the John Yoos of the world—saying, "I think all of those prior memos," referring to the John Yoo memos, "were done—did not violate professional responsibility," because it's recognized that currently there's an investigation going on of John Yoo, and I think it's very—and Bradbury, himself—and I think it's very likely that that's going to come out and say certainly disciplinary, if not disbarment, for those guys. So I think Yoo is facing that and, as I said, prosecution. . . .

Prosecutions for Corruption?

Goodman: And are there other countries that are pursuing a possible prosecution against any of these Bush administration officials?

Ratner: Well, I think right now what's happening is they're going to wait and see what Obama does. If Obama doesn't do anything in the next few months, I think there's going to be a huge push in Europe. At the same time, there is stuff going on in Europe, and that's—when there's conduct or illegalities on the country itself, they don't have to wait for the United States. So, you have an investigation, that we've talked about here, in Italy of the CIA agents going on who kidnapped an Egyptian cleric off the street. In Spain, you have a—

Goodman: Explain that. You have CIA officers being tried *in absentia* in Italy.

Ratner: That's correct. There were twenty-four CIA officers involved in a conspiracy to kidnap an Egyptian cleric off the streets of Milan. There's an independent prosecutor in Italy who has been running a trial now for probably a year or more, in which testimony is being taken on what those CIA agents have done. I think there's arrest warrants issued for a number of those people throughout Europe. So that's one relatively successful effort in Italy. And again, if you look at it, they actually kidnapped someone and violated the sovereignty of Italy, so they went after them.

Spain, likewise, has an investigation going on with a court, a judge, because the rendition flights landed in Majorca, they landed in Spain. And so, Spain looked, and its territory has been violated. So that's going on.

But I think, overall, what we're seeing here is—I mean, from my perspective, we're seeing actually more push for prosecutions than I actually expected, that the American public, it seems, is not really giving the sort of Obama line, "Let's look forward and not backward." Of course, to me, prosecutions is looking forward, because that's how you prevent torture in the future. So I think we're seeing a much greater push. I do think, though, that, as I want to say, that the combination of the memos and Leahy should just really send a message to America that we've got to make these guys accountable.

Exploiting Clients and Third World Countries

Ron Scherer and Brendan Conway

Journalists Brendan Conway and Ron Scherer both write for The Christian Science Monitor.

Using financier Robert Allen Stanford as the prime example, Conway and Scherer demonstrate the corruption and exploitation of clients in the financial markets. In February 2009, Stanford came under investigation for fraud and possible ties to money laundering for a Mexican drug cartel. Twelve years prior to his fraud accusation, Stanford was asked by Antigua's then-prime minister, Lester Bird, to help with the rewrite of the nation's money-laundering regulations. In June 2009, Stanford was indicted on 21 counts of conspiracy, fraud, bribery, and obstruction of justice as part of an alleged scheme to bilk investors through certificates of deposit issued by a bank on the Caribbean island of Antigua. He has pleaded not guilty.

Until 2000, Robert Allen Stanford had no record of giving money to anyone in Washington. But then the Clinton administration introduced legislation to crack down on international money laundering.

Suddenly Mr. Stanford, whose company ran a bank in Antigua, made a lot of friends, spreading money to both political parties and their leaders. The legislation languished in a Senate committee until the terrorist attacks of 9/11 convinced Congress it needed to act.

Stanford, accused by the US Securities and Exchange Commission (SEC) of an $8 billion fraud, continued to give money to scores of members of Congress, as well as the Obama presidential campaign.

The contributions, along with those from accused swindler Bernard Madoff, once again raise questions about the relationship of the rich and sometimes fraudulent to America's lawmakers.

The campaign contributions are "one vehicle to try to influence and skew policy," says Sheila Krumholz, executive director of the Center for Responsive Politics (CRP), which follows campaign contributions. "Often the efforts are too brazen."

Gaining Attention

In Stanford's case, since 2000 he, his company, or its employees have delivered $2.4 million to political operations, according to Ms. Krumholz. Stanford and his wife personally gave $931,000.

Although he donated to politicians of both parties, 65 percent of his donations went to Democrats, including $31,750 from Stanford, his family, and employees to the presidential campaign of Barack Obama.

"It's a lot of money when you consider 99 percent of the public doesn't even give $200," the amount needed to gain the attention of the Federal Election Commission, Krumholz says. "It makes him a big player."

In fact, politicians of both parties have been scrambling to distance themselves from the scandal. An Obama aide says the $4,600 contribution from Stanford himself has been donated to charity. Sen. Bill Nelson (D) of Florida is going one step further, shedding money that came from Stanford or his employees.

"Bill has told his campaign he wants every thin dime associated with Stanford returned to a charity or used in some way that could help folks who were deceived by this guy," a Nelson aide says in an e-mail.

Under Investigation

The same thing happened after the Madoff financial scandal broke. Mr. Madoff and his wife were also contributors to the political process, giving $238,200 since 1991, according to the CRP. His own donations, plus those of his firm, total nearly $1 million.

Two of the largest recipients, Sens. Ron Wyden (D) of Oregon ($13,000) and Charles Schumer (D) of New York ($12,000), say they have donated the money to charity.

Federal authorities accuse Stanford of "massive" fraud centering on high-interest-rate certificates of deposit (CDs). According to the SEC, in recent weeks the Stanford Financial Group has quoted rates as high as 10 percent on a five-year CD, more than twice the highest current US rate, which bankrate.com says is less than 4 percent.

Stanford, who has not been charged with any crime, may have yet more pressing concerns. According to an ABC News report, federal authorities are investigating the banker regarding money laundering for a Mexican drug cartel. The network, on its website, says one of Stanford's private planes was detained last year by Mexican officials, who found suspicious checks that might be drug related.

Stanford's Role in Antigua

Stanford, who was born in Mexia, Texas, has dual citizenship in the US and the Caribbean nation of Antigua and Barbuda, the site of his international banking operations.

In the past, the Caribbean island nation has been in the cross hairs over its money-laundering rules.

Stanford Financial Group chairman Robert Allen Stanford leaves the Bob Casey Federal Courthouse after a bond appeal hearing in Houston, Texas, in 2009. Stanford, who has been indicted on twenty-one counts of conspiracy, wire fraud, mail fraud, and obstruction of justice, is a prime example of corruption in today's financial market. © Dave Einsel/ Getty Images.

Twelve years ago, after the US imposed sanctions on the island, then-Prime Minister Lester Bird asked Stanford to help oversee a rewrite of Antigua's money-laundering regulations.

"The embassy described it as record-gate or file-gate," recalls Jonathan Winer, then deputy assistant secretary of State for international law enforcement. "Stanford took over the records of the offshore bank regulator, created the rules for cleaning it up, and drafted the legislation. None of us had ever seen anything like this before," says Mr. Winer, now a senior vice president at APCO International in Washington, a global consulting firm.

Stuart Eizenstat, who was deputy secretary of the Treasury from 1999 to 2001, recalls the notoriety of Antigua as it failed to improve. Antigua appeared on a Treasury "name and shame" list during that period, but, unlike other countries, Antigua was not "shamed."

"That list included Russia, Liechtenstein, Panama, Israel, and Antigua among countries not up to international standards," says Mr. Eizenstat, now head of the international practice at the law firm Covington & Burling in Washington.

"Most of the other countries did change their rules, but not Antigua," he says.

Stanford Helps Stall Money-Laundering Legislation

Cutting down on money laundering and financial fraud became a significant interest of Rep. Mike Rogers (R) of Michigan, a former FBI agent. He introduced legislation to improve the ability of state and federal agencies to share information. With the support of the Clinton administration, it passed the House.

But when the bill reached the US Senate, it stalled.

The public-interest lobbying group Public Citizen became curious about what happened. It found Stanford had given contributions to the "soft money" accounts of then-Sen. Tom

Daschle (D) of South Dakota, who was Senate minority leader, as well as other key legislators and both political parties.

"What we concluded was that it was his soft-money contribution, aimed at killing the money-laundering legislation, that got the bill killed," says Steve Weissman, then at Public Citizen, now associate director for policy at the Campaign Finance Institute in Washington.

Representative Rogers knew from his experience at the FBI that something needed to be done, says a spokeswoman.

"If the law had been adopted, it would have surely impacted transparency and made it easier to prevent the fraud cases we're seeing now," she says, quoting him.

Justice Politicized

David Iglesias with Davin Seay

David Iglesias was a United States attorney in New Mexico from 2001 to 2007, when he and other U.S. attorneys were dismissed presumably for political reasons. Davin Seay is a professional writer.

In the following selection, Iglesias discusses an investigation into political corruption, which continued into 2009 and involved the firing without cause of seven United States attorneys in 2006, himself included. These attorneys were dismissed by then attorney general of the United States, Alberto Gonzales, nicknamed "Fredo" by President George W. Bush. U.S. attorneys can only be fired for two reasons: fraudulent and unethical behavior, and incompetence. Yet none of these attorneys were ever charged with either of these. They lost their jobs when at least one senator and others in the administration became infuriated when the attorneys prosecuted cases that the administration wanted ignored for political reasons, and when they failed to prosecute cases that the administration wanted tried. During congressional hearings, Gonzales refused to convey information, damning himself, and leading to his own dismissal.

By the end of March 2007, the scandal that had engulfed my life and the lives of my colleagues had transitioned from the personal realm into a larger historical context. I would, of course, continue my involvement in getting the story out, even as I recognized that my days as a point person for the Justice League were drawing to a close. My wife and children once again become my top priority: I needed to find a job.

David Iglesias with Davin Seay, *In Justice: Inside the Scandal That Rocked the Bush Administration*. Hoboken, NJ: John Wiley & Sons, Inc., 2008. This material is used by permission of John Wiley & Sons, Inc.

Not all of the attention that I received was favorable or even pleasant. My role as betrayer of the Republican Party was writ large for some, especially in the tight, fierce circles of New Mexico politics. Members of a shadowy group calling itself New Mexicans for Honest Courts took it upon themselves to launch a one-minute radio ad campaign excoriating me for taking "taxpayer-funded junkets around the world." "David Iglesias," the spot concluded. "He still can't figure out why he was fired. Come on, David. Isn't it obvious?" . . .

Poisoned by Partisanship

If the point was to intimidate me into a cowed silence, they were wasting their time. The fact was the story had grown way beyond me or any of us, for that matter. . . . It was an awful sight to behold, as, one after the other, important people in powerful positions struggled to save their reputations. But it was also a greatly satisfying purge of the political bloodstream, which had been poisoned by partisanship. Despite the best efforts of those at [the] Main Justice [offices in Washington, D.C.] and the White House to prove otherwise, the system was actually working.

Like many historical accounts, the dénouement of this unhappy chapter in the annals of American law and justice became a series of footnotes that trailed off without reaching a final, formal conclusion. Calls for the resignation of Attorney General Alberto Gonzales, beginning with such staunch Republican legislators as John Sununu, Gordon Smith, Dana Rohrbacher, and Paul Gillmor, resounded within two weeks of our committee appearances. Before the month was out, the White House had presented to the restive lawmakers a startling compromise to their demand for records and testimony from key administration officials, including William Kelley, Harriet Miers, and, most urgently, Karl Rove. The conditions for their cooperation were, simply put, stunning: all testimony would be in closed-door sessions; no transcript would be kept of the meeting; and the White House staff members would not be sworn in. Any trial lawyer will tell you that this type of testimony is worthless since you cannot use it to challenge a later statement.

This unprecedented act of political chutzpah was underscored the same day, March 20, when President George W. Bush held a press conference to, among other things, reaffirm his support for the attorney general and vow to resist any subpoenas of his staff by the House or Senate Judiciary Committees. . . .

Who Was Responsible?

One of the most commonly asked questions heard in the aftermath of the scandal was whether Gonzales was actually responsible for what happened on his watch or was, rather, only an obedient pawn in political machinations that reached, perhaps, into the Oval Office itself. I certainly can understand the reasons behind such speculation, as part of the deep and lingering mistrust of government since the Watergate era, when suspicions of presidential involvement in criminal activity ran deep and it was imperative to pin down what the chief executive knew and when he knew it.

But the correlation goes only so far. Who was really guilty of this concerted attempt to co-opt the Justice Department for political ends? It's certainly easy, as far as it goes, to point the finger at the hapless attorney general. It was his job to protect the integrity of the institution he led, and in that respect, Alberto Gonzales was a miserable failure. But does that analysis go far enough? In the case of Karl Rove—who was charged with the weighty responsibility of being the president's domestic policy adviser—certainly not.

But what about Bush himself? There is no question that he had been apprised of complaints by Republican politicians regarding many of the U.S. Attorneys who were subsequently fired. But was it his responsibility to investigate such matters?

Of course not. That was the attorney general's job. Yet was Bush, by hiring someone as pliant and blindly loyal as Gonzales, somehow culpable in the resulting catastrophe? I think it depends on when, exactly, benign neglect becomes malicious intent. Bush set a standard that placed allegiance to him above all else, and Gonzales met that standard at every turn. From that fundamental premise, all else proceeded.

Gonzales's Testimony

As personal as my emotions might have been regarding my former superior, I know that I had in common the same feelings as most Americans when I watched the dismaying, deceiving, and ultimately depressing performance the attorney general of the United States gave before the Senate Judiciary Committee on April 19, 2007. It became, in its aftermath, an enduring moment of deep embarrassment, even shame, for our nation to watch its chief law enforcement officer dodge and deny the truth, even as he willingly cast himself as both incompetent and arrogant in order to protect an administration that, in the final reckoning, did not deserve his fealty. Yet his appearance that day was as infuriating as it was mortifying. Gonzales greeted even the sharpest attacks on his honesty and integrity with the same bland, slightly bemused expression, as if, for the life of him, he couldn't figure out what all the fuss was about. The increasing frustration and utter disbelief expressed by his questioners were deflected by a kind of search-me smirk that never wavered. In some unfathomable way, Gonzales had made peace with the process of being torn apart, secure in the knowledge that at the end of the day, his most important allegiance—to the president—had remained inviolate.

What showed through instead was an utter disregard, bordering on contempt, for the committee, its authority, and its mission. Before the hearing broke for lunch, Gonzales had answered nearly sixty questions posed to him in exactly the same way: "I do not recall." When pressed by Senator Ted Kennedy as to the procedure for the firings, Gonzales suggested with a long-suffering air that since the committee had already interviewed most of his aides, the senators now knew more about the dismissals than he did. . . .

So it went. Under intense questioning from Chairman Pat Leahy about the timing and the intent of my forced resignation, the attorney general, while admitting that he "accepted the recommendation," at the same time insisted that he was "not responsible for compiling the list." "I was not surprised," he added, "that Mr. Iglesias was recommended to me, because I had heard about concerns . . . from Senator Domenici."

"And Karl Rove?" Leahy pressed.

Yes, Gonzales admitted, "I heard concerns raised by Mr. Rove."

When asked to elaborate on the reasons I had lost the attorney general's confidence, as he had stated in his *USA Today* editorial on March 7, [2007,] the judge recalled a conversation he'd had in the fall of 2005 with Pete Domenici. "[H]e called me and said something to the effect that Mr. Iglesias was in over his head."

"My question," interrupted Leahy, "was when and why did he lose *your* confidence."

"What I instructed Mr. Sampson to do was consult with people in the department . . . ," Gonzales stammered.

"When and why did he lose your confidence?" the senator asked for the third time.

He never did get an answer, and it's hard to discount the possibility that there was no answer to get. The attorney general didn't have the faintest idea when and why he had lost confidence in me. Nor was he willing to admit that any of the reasons proffered to date had been insufficient. Clearly, I had not lost the confidence of Gonzales, as evidenced by his non-responsive answers. He clearly had not expressed any concerns when he visited my office in August 2006, just months before my name was added to the list. I had lost the confidence of Domenici, who had taken the counsel of what author J.R.R. Tolkien would have called his "worm tongues."

"When, how, and by whom did the 'absentee landlord' rationale for replacing Mr. Iglesias arise?" Leahy continued.

"That rationale was not in my mind," Gonzales responded, "when I accepted the recommendation. . . ."

By the conclusion of that long and exasperating day, Senator Charles Schumer attempted, as best he could, to sum up the dispiriting juggling act the committee had just witnessed. "[We] laid out the burden of proof for you to meet, to answer questions directly and fully," the lawmaker commenced, "You've answered 'I don't know' or 'I can't recall' to close to a hundred questions. You're not familiar with much of the workings of your own department. And we still don't have convincing explanations of the who, why, and when in regard to the firings. . . . You haven't met any of these three tests. I don't see the point of another round of questions. And I urge you to reexamine your performance and, for the good of the department and the good of the country step down." . . .

That moment of realization would, in due course, arrive, albeit much earlier for most Americans than for the attorney general himself. Four months later, and much longer than any who had witnessed the debacle in the hearing room might have given him, Attorney General Alberto Gonzales announced his resignation. The pleasure of the president was no longer served, and the highest-ranking official to lose his job in the aftermath of the scandal was cut loose as the administration circled its wagons a little tighter.

James Comey's Testimony

James Comey, the former deputy attorney general under both [John] Ashcroft and Gonzales, saw it from another perspective. His riveting testimony on May 15 before a Senate Judiciary Committee—still immersed in the investigation and the efforts to shake loose more information from Main Justice and the White House—was one of the most damning indictments yet, not only of Gonzales, but of an entire administration that had indeed lost its moral rudder. . . .

There was perhaps no lower ebb in the whole story than Comey's description of the attempt by Gonzales, who was then White House counsel, to get John Ashcroft to sign off on a controversial warrantless surveillance program, while the attorney general lay virtually at death's door in a hospital intensive-care room. It seemed that men who would stoop to such levels would hardly have qualms about firing dedicated public servants, an observation that Jim Comey stirringly underscored by telling the committee that he was unwilling to "sit by and watch good people smeared."

One by one, and for the record, Senator Arlen Specter sounded off our names.

"Dan Bogden."

"Dan Bogden was an excellent U.S. Attorney."

"As to John McKay and the competency of his performance?"

"Again, it was excellent in my experience."

"And as to Paul Charlton, Arizona U.S. Attorney?"

"The same." Comey paused. "I don't want to make it look like I love everybody, but I did like him a great deal."

Senator Specter waited for the laughter to die down before continuing his roll call. "And David Iglesias, U.S. Attorney for New Mexico."

"Same thing. I dealt with him quite a bit, both as a peer and as his superior, and had a high opinion of him. I thought he did a very good job."

Comey later recalled to me the moment when he first knew that his beloved Justice Department had been hijacked. "I was sitting with my wife watching [deputy attorney general] Paul McNulty's testimony on TV," he told me. "When he claimed that everyone had been let go for performance-related reasons, I turned to her and said, 'They just lit a powder keg.'"

The fuse to that keg may have been long, but it came to an end that April day in the hearing room when Fredo fell on his sword as the nation watched aghast. But to hear John McKay tell it, the fuse still has a ways to go. McKay, who currently teaches constitutional law, law of terrorism, and national security law at Seattle University, recently prepared an article for the school law review, titled "Train Wreck at the Justice Department." In it, he presents a compelling case for obstruction of justice charges to be brought against Gonzales. . . .

Ethics and the U.S. Legal System

What McKay left unsaid was that such a pursuit might well lead beyond the halls of the Justice Department and into other, more secretive, realms of government. It's hard to know whether the damage done by our forced resignations was a factor in the departure of Karl Rove four days after Gonzales made his own farewell announcement. In the Byzantine labyrinths of power through which Rove moved, there may never be anything as simple as cause and effect. But it doesn't really matter. Comey's analogy of the lit fuse may extend a little further still. Out of office, Rove is hardly off the minds of the lawmakers who are still seeking answers to those "mysteries without any clues." Even as the Office of the Inspector General prepares its long-gestating report on the possible legal and ethical violations of the firings, Democrats on the Senate Judiciary, Committee, as recently as December 2007, pushed forward with a resolution to hold the White House in contempt of Congress for failing to provide a long list of subpoenaed information and witnesses in the investigation.

At that top of that list is Karl Rove, and for him and others, the final verdict has yet to be rendered. Within days of the one-year anniversary of our firings, the Senate Judiciary Committee voted to hold Rove in contempt of Congress for refusing to cooperate in its probe of the firings, in the process rejecting the administration's claim of executive privilege for withholding documents and testimony. It's the opening salvo in the next stage of an ongoing battle being waged over one of the fundamental principles of the American experiment: the separation of powers.

It is, of course, in the success or the failure of that experiment that the true significance of the scandal lies. It was not about me losing my job, however painful that might have been; nor was it about the unprecedented act of forcing out a group of highly competent and ethical federal prosecutors for base political reasons, however unfair that might have been. The deepest implications of the disaster at Main Justice are not of partisan politics, nor are they of transient liberal or conservative issues. Rather, at their molecular core, they are issues of illegality and unconstitutionality. I spoke out because I could never get over the insurmountable fact that what had happened to me was wrong and that it would be repeated to future U.S. Attorneys unless I spoke out.

The scandal was a wrenching but necessary object lesson about the need to maintain the independence of the prosecutor and the consequences of attempting to politicize the criminal justice system at the highest levels. A politicized prosecutor is anathema to anyone who has read the Constitution or studied American history. As McKay eloquently stated in an analysis for the *Washington State Bar Association* magazine, "What's at stake here is prosecutorial independence from partisan politics and renewed dedication to fair and impartial justice which is tempered by compassion." . . .

Motives Behind Firings

To the Gonzales Justice Department, U.S. Attorneys were mere political appointees, not impartial and nonpolitical agents of justice to be protected from the capricious winds of Capitol

Hill. It was as if we were mere summer help with law degrees, to be moved about the appointment chessboard by the likes of Karl Rove as he sought the Holy Grail of a permanent Republican majority in government.

In the end, the Justice Department debacle proved the resiliency of the American system of checks and balances. An emboldened House and Senate sought to reveal just how much partisan politics contaminated a department with a long and proud history of staying out of politics. The results were ugly. If the executive privilege claim will be resolved, Congress should get a full accounting of who actually ordered the terminations and why. Only then will the system's checks and balances be seen for what they truly are—not inconvenient obstacles to political ends, but a necessary expedient against an ascendant executive branch that was bent on expanding its wartime powers to areas that have nothing to do with the legitimate role of the commander in chief of the armed forces.

Power is a terrible thing to behold if it is not restrained by fairness and decency. Former attorney general and Supreme Court justice Robert Jackson said it best, "[T]he citizen's safety lies in the prosecutor who tempers zeal with human kindness, who seeks truth and not victims, who serves the law and not factional purposes, and who approaches his task with humility."

This administration's Justice Department was driven by political hubris, not by the basic concepts of fairness and fair play that are precious to us all. The leadership was not committed to the rule of law, but to the rule of politics. And in the gladiatorial world of Washington, D.C., politics, the leadership at the Justice Department found out the hard truth to this eternal principle: you reap what you sow.

For Further Discussion

1. Discuss the aspects of William Shakespeare's life and the Elizabethan world he lived in as they seem to have shaped the topic of corruption in *Hamlet*.

2. There is obviously political corruption in Denmark in *Hamlet*. Investigate how that has resulted in inner corruption. Consult Spurgeon and Gurr.

3. Has Claudius's and Gertrude's corruption driven Hamlet mad, or is he pretending to be mad? Consult Bradley and McLauchlan.

4. Debate the idea that Hamlet is as guilty as Claudius. Consult Traversi, Knight, Bradley, and Kitto.

5. Discuss the idea, using contemporary examples, of how political/social corruption can spread like a disease.

For Further Reading

William Shakespeare, *Coriolanus*. The Arden Shakespeare Complete Works. Edited by Richard Proudfoot, Ann Thompson, and David Scott Kastan. London: Arden Shakespeare, 2000.

————, *Julius Caesar*. The Arden Shakespeare Complete Works. Edited by Richard Proudfoot, Ann Thompson, and David Scott Kastan. London: Arden Shakespeare, 2000.

————, *King Henry IV, Part 1*. The Arden Shakespeare Complete Works. Edited by Richard Proudfoot, Ann Thompson, and David Scott Kastan. London: Arden Shakespeare, 2000.

————, *King Henry VIII*. The Arden Shakespeare Complete Works. Edited by Richard Proudfoot, Ann Thompson, and David Scott Kastan. London: Arden Shakespeare, 2000.

————, *King John*. The Arden Shakespeare Complete Works. Edited by Richard Proudfoot, Ann Thompson, and David Scott Kastan. London: Arden Shakespeare, 2000.

————, *King Lear*. The Arden Shakespeare Complete Works. Edited by Richard Proudfoot, Ann Thompson, and David Scott Kastan. London: Arden Shakespeare, 2000.

————, *King Richard III*. The Arden Shakespeare Complete Works. Edited by Richard Proudfoot, Ann Thompson, and David Scott Kastan. London: Arden Shakespeare, 2000.

————, *Troilus and Cressida*. The Arden Shakespeare Complete Works. Edited by Richard Proudfoot, Ann Thompson, and David Scott Kastan. London: Arden Shakespeare, 2000.

Bibliography

Books

Peter Alexander   *Hamlet: Father and Son.* Oxford, UK:
Clarendon Press, 1955.

Fredson Bowers   *Elizabethan Revenge Tragedy.*
Princeton, NJ: Princeton University
Press, 1940.

Avi Erlich   *Hamlet's Absent Father.* Princeton,
NJ: Princeton University Press, 1977.

Northrup Frye   *Fools of Time: Studies in
Shakespearean Tragedy.* Toronto:
University of Toronto Press, 1967.

Roland M. Frye   *The Renaissance "Hamlet": Issues and
Responses in 1600.* Princeton, NJ:
Princeton University Press, 1984.

Felix Gross   *The Seizure of Political Power.* New
York: Philosophical Library, 1958.

Bertram L. Joseph   *Conscience and the King: A Study of
"Hamlet."* London: Chatto and
Windus, 1953.

Alexander Nigel   *Poison, Play, and Duel: A Study in
"Hamlet."* Lincoln: University of
Nebraska Press, 1971.

Greg Palast   *The Best Democracy Money Can Buy.*
New York: Penguin, 2003.

Eleanor Prosser   *Hamlet and Revenge.* Stanford, CA:
                     Stanford University Press, 1971.

Allen Raymond   *Confessions of a Republican Operative:
                     How to Rig an Election.* New York:
                     Simon and Schuster, 2008.

Peter C. Rollins   *Shakespeare's Theories of Blood,
and Alan Smith,   Character, and Class.* New York: Peter
eds.   Lang, 2001.

Gary Taylor   *Reinventing Shakespeare: A Cultural
                     History from the Restoration to the
                     Present.* New York: Weidenfeld and
                     Nicolson, 1989.

Periodicals

Richard D. Altick   "Hamlet and the Odor of Mortality,"
                     Shakespeare Quarterly, vol. 5, 1954.

J. Anthony   "'His Quarry Cries on Haucke': Is
Burton   This Shakespeare's Own Judgment on
                     the Meaning of *Hamlet?" Upstart
                     Crow,* vol. 11, 1991.

Monica Davey   "Blagojevich Denies Guilt, This Time
                     Officially," *New York Times,* April 15,
                     2009.

Alan C. Dessen   "Hamlet's Poisoned Sword: A Study
                     in Dramatic Imagery," *Shakespeare
                     Studies,* vol. 5, 1969.

R.A. Foakes   "Hamlet and the Court of Elsinore,"
                     Shakespeare Survey, vol. 9, 1956.

James V. Holleran   "Maimed Funeral Rites in *Hamlet*," *English Literary Renaissance*, vol. 19, 1989.

Geoffrey Hughes   "The Tragedy of a Revenger's Loss of Conscience: A Study of *Hamlet*," *English Studies*, vol. 57, 1976.

Jane Mayer   "Contract Sport: What Did the Vice-President Do for Halliburton?" *New Yorker*, February 16 & 23, 2004.

Ramesh Ponnuru and Richard Lowry   "The Grim Truth," *National Review*, November 19, 2007.

Mark Rose   "Hamlet and the Shape of Revenge," *English Literary Renaissance*, vol. 1, 1971.

Thomas F. Van Laan   "Ironic Reversal in *Hamlet*," *Studies in English Literature, 1500–1900*, vol. 6, no. 2, 1966.

Index

A

Act of Uniformity, 9
Adams, John, 120
Andrews, John F., 16–26
Anglican Church, 57
Antigua, 148, 150
Arden, Edward, 39
Aristophanes, 121
Aristotle, 120–121
Armin, Robert, 23
Arnold, Matthew, 123
Ashcroft, John, 158

B

Beauty imagery, 65–66
Bird, Lester, 150
Blackstone, William, 110
Bogden, Dan, 158
Boleyn, Anne, 57
Borromeo, Charles, 30
Bradley, A.C., 43–51
Brandeis, Louis, 120
Brook, Daniel, 115–124
Burbage, James, 23
Burbage, Richard, 21, 23, 34, 36
Bush, George W., 129, 138, 154–155

C

Cabela's, 118
Calhoun, John C., 121
Catholicism, 9, 30–31, 38–39
Cerjan, Paul, 129, 134
Charlton, Paul, 158

Chatterjee, Pratap, 128–137
Cheney, Dick, 137
Childhood, of Shakespeare, 16–20, 28–29
Church of England, 9, 18, 57
Claudius (*Hamlet*)
    corruption of, 44–45, 49, 68–69, 76–81
    Hamlet and, 76, 78
    as human, 85–87
    marriage between Gertrude and, 54–57, 58
    morality of, 87–88
    sickness imagery and, 63–64
    violation of natural order by, 92–93
Comey, James, 157–159
Condell, Henry, 25
Confessions of an Economic Hit Man (Perkins), 125–127
Conscience, 71–72
Conway, Brendan, 146–151
Corporate socialism, 117–119
Corruption
    in Bush administration, 144–145, 152–161
    of Claudius, 44–45, 49, 68–69, 76–81
    economic inequality and, 115–124
    in financial markets, 146–151
    generational conflict and, 107–113
    government, 137, 144–145, 152–161
    of Hamlet, 82–89
    insanity and, 68–73

in international corporations,
125–127
of love, 79, 84, 99–106
of natural order, 92–93
parallels between Elizabethan
England and *Hamlet*'s Denmark, 52–60
Pentagon and, 128–137
as pervasive disease, 74–81
political, 152–161
of Polonius, 46–47
of reason, 90–98
sickness imagery and, 62–67
Crum, Tom, 131

D

Daschle, Tom, 150–151
Davies, Richard, 41
Death, 84–85, 99–100
Democracy, 121–123
Democracy Now!, 138–145
Denmark (*Hamlet*)
corruption in, 43–51
elective monarchy in, 53
evil in, 101–102
political crisis in, 54–55
political marriages in, 55–57
welfare of, 89
Devereux, Robert, 9
DeYoung, Marie, 133
Dictatorship, 143
Disease imagery, 62–67, 74–81
Divine justice, 50–51
Divine right of kings, 59
Domenici, Pete, 156
Drama, art of, 37

E

Earl of Essex, 22
Earl of Southampton, 9, 39

Eccleston, Christopher, *38*
Economic inequality
consequences of, 123–124
corruption and, 115–124
democracy and, 121–123
Edward I, 57, 58
Eizenstat, Stuart, 150
Elizabeth I, 9, 22, 37, 57–59
Elizabethan England
murder plots in, 58–59
political context of, 53–54
political marriages in, 55–57
view of *Hamlet* in, 60
Espionage, 138–145
Ethics, 159–160
Evil, 101–102

F

Financial market corruption, 146–
151
First Folio, 25–26
Foreboding, 75
Fortinbras (*Hamlet*), 76, 92
Franks, Tommy, 129, 133
Fraud, 146–151
Free Lunch (Johnston), 116–119,
123
Friedman, Milton, 121

G

Geha, Camille, 131
Generational conflict, 107–113
Gertrude (*Hamlet*)
corruption of love and, 79
marriage between Claudius
and, 54–57, 58
Ophelia and, 105–106
sickness imagery and, 62–63
Ghost (*Hamlet*), 50–51, 74–75, 94

Globe Theatre, 9, 23, 37
Gonzales, Alberto, 152–161
Government contracts, 129–137
Government corruption, 137, 144–145, 152–161
Grazia, Margreta de, 107–113
Green, Joseph, 27
Greene, Robert, 36
Greider, William, 121
Guild Chapel, 19–20
Guildenstern (*Hamlet*), 93
Gurr, Andrew, 68–73

H

Halliburton, 128–137
Hamilton, Alexander, 121
Hamlet (*Hamlet*)
    Claudius and, 76, 78
    corruption of, 82–89
    degeneration of, 93–95
    on divine right of kings, 59
    inner and outer worlds of, 69–70
    inner conflict within, 90–98
    melancholy of, 43–44, 47, 49, 83–84
    misery of, 83
    morality of, 70–71, 87–88
    Ophelia and, 102–106
    succession to throne and, 108–110
Hamlet (Shakespeare)
    background of writing of, 9–10, 34
    conflict within, 80–81
    death in, 84–85, 99–100
    generational conflict in, 107–113
    hand of Providence in, 49–50
    insanity in, 68–73, 112

murder plots in, 58–59
politics in, 52–60
remakes of, *47*
as revenge tragedy, 11
sickness imagery in, 61–67, 74–81
turning point of, 45–46
writing of, 34
See also specific characters
Hamlett, Katherine, 30, 34
Hankins, John Erskine, 52–60
Harrison, G.B., 35–41
Hathaway, Anne, 20–21, 32, 35–36
Heminge, John, 25
Henry VI (Shakespeare), 36
Henry VII, 56, 57
Henry VIII, 9, 53, 57–58
Henry VIII (Shakespeare), 10, 57
Henslowe, Philip, 23, 36
Holland, Peter, 27–34
Horatio (*Hamlet*), 59, 75, 97–98
Hurricane Katrina, 132–133

I

Idealism, 91–92
Iglesias, David, 152–161
Images
    recurrent, 61–67
    of sickness and disease, 61–67, 74–81
Income inequality, 119–121
Industrial capitalism, 122–123
Inheritance, 110
Inns of Court, 22
Insanity, 68–73, 112
Iraq War, 129–137

J

Jackson, Robert, 161
James I, 37, 53
James VI, 58
Jefferson, Thomas, 120
Johnston, David Cay, 116–119, 123
Jordan, John, 31, 38
Justice Department, 152–161

K

Katherine of Aragon, 57
KBR, 129–137
Kempe, Will, 23, 36
Kennedy, John F., 129
Kennedy, Ted, 156
King Lear (Shakespeare), 11
King's Men, 37
King's New School, 19–20
Kingsworth, Paul, 125–127
Kitto, H.D.F., 99–106
Knight, G. Wilson, 82–89
Krumholz, Sheila, 147
Kyd, Thomas, 11, 34

L

Laertes (*Hamlet*), 48, 80, 89, 112
Laissez-faire, 118–119
Leahy, Patrick, 139–140, 156–157
Lesar, David, 131–132, 134
London, England, 21–22, 33
Lord Chamberlain's Men, 22–23, 33, 36–37
Love
    corruption of, 79, 84, 99–106
    degeneration of, 94–95
    as goodness, 100–101
Lucy, Thomas, 36

M

Macbeth (Shakespeare), 11, 50
Machiavelli, Niccolò, 121
Madness, 68–73, 112
Madoff, Bernard, 147, 148
Malone, Edmond, 30–31, 38–39
Manningham, John, 21
Marlowe, Christopher, 33
Marriage
    political, 55–57
    religion and, 57–58
    Shakespeare's, 20–21, 32, 35–36
Mary, Queen of Scots (Mary Stuart), 53, 56, 58–59
Mazon, Jeff, 133
McKay, John, 158, 159, 160
McLauchlan, Juliet, 90–98
McNulty, Paul, 158–159
Military outsourcing, 129–137
Monarchy, 53–54
Money laundering, 146–151
Morality, 70–71, 87–88
Multinational corporations, 125–127
Murder plots, 58–59

N

National Committee of La Raza (NCLR), 136
Natural order, corruption of, 92–93
Nelson, Bill, 147–148

O

Obama, Barack, 145, 147
Ophelia (*Hamlet*)
    beauty imagery and, 65–66

childlike nature of, 111–112
death of, 105
on Hamlet, 95
insanity of, 48, 72–73, 80, 112
inspiration for, *30*, 34
love between Hamlet and,
   100, 102–106

P

Padilla, Jose, 143
Partisanship, 153–154
Pentagon, 128–137
Perkins, John, 125–127
Personifications, 65–66
Pinochet, Augusto, 121
Poison, 99–100
Political corruption, 152–161
Political marriages, 55–57
Politics, 52–60
The Politics of Inequality
  (Thompson), 119–124
Polonius (*Hamlet*)
  corruption of, 46–47
  death of, 101
  exploitation of love by, 100–
    101
  family of, 78
  poison within, 80
Primogeniture, 110
Protestant Reformation, 9
Providence, 49–50

Q

Queen's Men, 33
Queen's Players, 31

R

Raleigh, Walter, 22
The Rape of Lucrece (Shakespeare),
  36

Ratner, Michael, 140–141
Reason, corruption of, 90–98
Religion, marriage and, 57–58
Renaissance, 11
Revenge tragedy, 11
Richard II (Shakespeare), 10
Richard III, 56
Ridgway, Matthew B., 128
Rogers, Mike, 150, 151
Root, Elihu, 129
Rosencrantz (*Hamlet*), 93
Rove, Karl, 156, 159–160, 161
Rumsfeld, Donald, 129, 137

S

Sadler, Hamnet, 32
Scherer, Ron, 146–151
Schumer, Charles, 148, 157
Seay, Davin, 152–161
Seneca, 11
Seventeenth century, 9
Seymour, Jane, 57
Shakespeare, Hamnet, 10, 32, 33–
  34, 36
Shakespeare, John, 9, 16–18, 28–
  31, 38–39
Shakespeare, Judith, 32, 36
Shakespeare, Mary Arden, 16, 17,
  28
Shakespeare, Susanna, 32, 36
Shakespeare, William
  birth of, 27–28
  childhood, 16–20, 28–29
  dark period for, 9–11
  education of, 18–20
  exposure of, to professional
    theatre, 31–32
  family of, 28–29
  final years of, 25–26

life of, 16–26
London career of, 21–22, 33, 36–37
marriage of, 20–21, 32, 35–36
painting of, *19*
as playwright, 24–25, 36–37
professional experience of, 22–25
religious affiliation of, 38, 39–41
Shinseki, Eric, 129
Sickness imagery, 61–67, 74–81
Somerville, John, 39
Spanish Armada, 22
The Spanish Tragedy (Kyd), 11
Specter, Arlen, 158
Spurgeon, Caroline F.E., 61–67
St. Paul's Cathedral, 21–22
Stanford, Robert Allen, 146–151, *149*
Steevens, George, 27
Stuart, Mary. *See* Mary, Queen of Scots (Mary Stuart)
Succession, law of, 108–110

T

Thatcher, Margaret, 121
Theatre companies, 31–32
Thompson, Michael, 119–124

Throne, succession to, 108–110
Torture, 138–145
Tower of London, 22
Traversi, Derek Antona, 74–81
Troilus and Cressida (Shakespeare), 10–11
Tudor, Mary, 9, 58
Twelfth Night (Shakespeare), 33

U

U.S. attorney firings, 152–161

V

Venus and Adonis (Shakespeare), 36, 39

W

Waxman, Henry, 133
Weissman, Steve, 151
Westminster Abbey, 22
Winer, Jonathan, 150
Wolfowitz, Paul, 129
Worcester's Men, 31
Wriothesley, Henry, 36
Wyden, Ron, 148

Y

Yoo, John, 144